Working Basics

20 Essential Skills
Student Workbook

© Copyright 1990-2003 The Paxen Group, Inc.

ISBN 10: 1-934350-02-8
ISBN 13: 978-1-934350-02-7

Developed by The Paxen Group, Inc.,

© Copyright 1990-2003, The Paxen Group, Inc. All rights reserved. No portion of this manual may be reproduced without the written consent of The Paxen Group, Inc.

800-247-2936

www.paxen.com

Table of Contents

Reading Work Schedules · 1
Reading Policy & Procedures Manuals · · · · · · · · · · · · · · · 9
Determining Sequential Events/Items · · · · · · · · · · · · · · · 15
Reading Abbreviations · 21
Reading Safety Warnings · 31
Reading Procedures · 39
Understanding Symbols · 47
Alphabetizing · 53
Finding Pages · 59
Adding Whole Numbers · 67
Subtracting Whole Numbers · 77
Multiplying Whole Numbers · 87
Dividing Whole Numbers · 101
Adding Decimals · 117
Subtracting Decimals · 123
Telling Time · 129
Allocating Time · 137
Identifying Work Related Problems · · · · · · · · · · · · · · · · 143
Reporting Emergencies · 151
Reading Advertisements · 157

Working Basics Essential Skills Competency Checklist
(from which agency may choose to document)

Client Name_____

RATING INSTRUCTIONS:

Observe the client as he or she demonstrates each competency. Assign a score of S (satisfactory) or U (unsatisfactory). Performance is considered satisfactory if:

1. The client completes the tasks correctly.
2. The client completes the tasks with minimal supervision.
3. Scores 70% or better on the Quiz.

The client must score a Satisfactory score on 70% (14 of 20) of these competencies to achieve competency in the Working Basics Essential Skills module.

Client's Initials	RATING (circle one)	COMPETENCY
	S U	1. Reading work schedules as demonstrated by 70% on SK7 quiz on pages 7-8.
	S U	2. Reading policy and procedure manuals as demonstrated by 70% on SK 8 quiz on pages 13-14.
	S U	3. Determining sequential events/items as demonstrated by 70% on SK 9 on page 19.
	S U	4. Reading abbreviations as demonstrated by 70% on SK 12 quiz on pages 29-30.
	S U	5. Reading safety warnings as demonstrated by 70% on SK 15 quiz on page 37.
	S U	6. Reading procedures as demonstrated by 70% on SK16 quiz on pages 45-46.
	S U	7. Understanding symbols as demonstrated by 70% on SK 20 quiz on page 51.
	S U	8. Alphabetizing as demonstrated by 70% on SK 21 quiz on pages 57-58.
	S U	9. Finding pages as demonstrated by 70% on SK 22 quiz on pages 65-66.
	S U	10. Adding whole numbers as demonstrated by 70% on SK30 quiz on pages 75-76.

continued next page

Working Basics

Client's Initials	RATING (circle one)	COMPETENCY
	S U	11. Subtracting whole numbers as demonstrated by 70% on SK 31 on pages 85-86.
	S U	12. Multiplying whole numbers as demonstrated by 70% on SK 32 quiz on Pages 99-100.
	S U	13. Dividing whole numbers as demonstrated by 70% on SK 33 quiz on pages 115-116.
	S U	14. Adding decimals as demonstrated by 70% on SK 38 quiz on pages 121-122.
	S U	15. Subtracting decimals as demonstrated by 70% on SK 39 quiz on pages 127-128
	S U	16. Telling time as demonstrated by 70% on SK 6 quiz on pages 135-136.
	S U	17. Allocating time as demonstrated by 70% on SK 85 quiz on pages 141-142.
	S U	18. Identifying work related problems as demonstrated by 70% on SK 94 quiz on pages 149-150.
	S U	19. Reporting emergencies as demonstrated by 70% on SK 95 quiz on page 155-156.
	S U	20. Reading advertisements as demonstrated by 70% on SK 101 quiz on page 163-164.

Total with Satisfactory Rating _____

The above named client has completed the Working Basics Essential Skills module. The rating will serve as documentation that each competency and its measurement criteria listed above were achieved.

Client Signature_____   Date_____

Instructor signs after final rating is completed. _____

                                                               Instructor Signature

Reading Work Schedules

Basic Skills
Module SK 7

Many entry level employees work a 9-to-5, every-Monday-through-every-Friday schedule. Those workers have no trouble remembering what days or hours to work. The work they do may vary, but the hours and days are always the same.

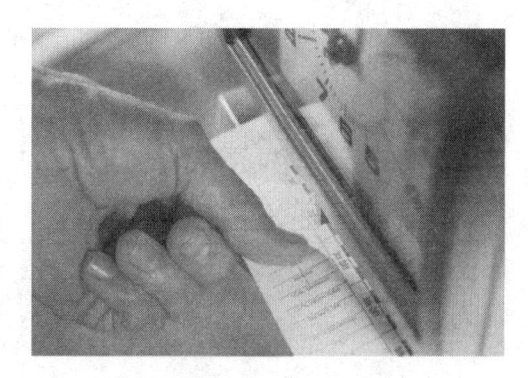

What about jobs where the employees work rotating schedules? Or how about around-the-clock operations where employees work different shifts depending on the day of the week? How are they supposed to know what days to work this week if they are different from the days they worked last week? The ability to read work schedules is the answer.

There are as many different types of work schedules as there are different types of jobs. First, let's discuss some entry level jobs that would require written work schedules. Nursing assistants, cashiers and data entry operators are three occupations where employees might work unusual hours. Can you list a few others?

Jobs Which Require Written Work Schedules

Working Basics

Today's technology has brought us to the point where workers must be available 24 hours a day. At midnight, more than seven million people in the United States are on their jobs! Night workers include bakers, cab drivers, police and sheriff deputies, hotel workers, toll collectors and disc jockeys. If these night workers work the same late hours on the same days each week, then they have no problem knowing and remembering when to report to work. But what happens when they work a rotating schedule such as four days on, two days off, four days on, etc.? What happens is a lot of missed work and probably a lost job - unless the employee carefully reads and follows a given work schedule.

Look at the work schedule pictured below:

MANAGER'S WEEKLY WORK SCHEDULE
STORE # 1073   PERIOD: MAY 1 - MAY 14

NAME	TUES	WED	THURS	FRI	SAT	SUN	MON
WEEK 1	5/1	5/2	5/3	5/4	5/5	5/6	5/7
Trudy	off	off	7am-3pm	7am-3pm	7am-12pm	3pm-11pm	off
Anthony	off	3pm-11pm	off	off	11pm-7am	11pm-7am	3pm-11pm
Keshia	11pm-7am	off	11pm-7am	11pm-5am	off	off	11pm-9am
WEEK 2	5/8	5/9	5/10	5/11	5/12	5/13	5/14
Trudy	off	10am-4pm	7am-3pm	7am-3pm	10am-6pm	off	off
Anthony	off	7am-7pm	7am-7pm	off	off	7am-7pm	7am-3pm
Keshia	3pm-11pm	off	off	3pm-11pm	3pm-11pm	11pm-7am	off

SK 7 Reading Work Schedules

This schedule is graphed for 2 weeks of a month. Notice the work week begins on a Tuesday. The three employees, Trudy, Anthony and Keshia work different hours on different days. They also have different days off. The times listed under each day of the week show you what time each person is supposed to start work and what time they are supposed to be finished with work. For example, in Week 1, Trudy has Tuesday and Wednesday off. On Thursday she works from 7:00 a.m. to 3:00 p.m. That is an 8 hour shift. She works these same hours on Friday, but on Saturday she is finished at 12:00. Sunday her hours are different again. That day she works from 3:00 in the afternoon until 11:00 at night. She doesn't work on Monday.

PRACTICE EXERCISE:

Using the work schedule from the previous page, answer the following practice questions:

1. Does Keshia have to work on the weekend of the first week?
Answer:
2. How many total hours does Anthony work on Thursday, May 10th?
Answer:
3. How many hours does Trudy work the second week?
Answer:
4. What time does Anthony need to be at work on May 8th?
Answer:
5. What time does Keshia leave work on Friday of the second week?
Answer:
6. Anthony has a date on May 11th, will he be able to make it?
Answer:
7. If Keshia arrives at work on May 3rd at 11:30 p.m., is she on time?
Answer:

Working Basics

For questions 8 - 13, use the work schedule below.

WORK SCHEDULE WEEK OF: January 26

Name	Shift	Meal Break	Mon	Tues	Wed	Thur	Fri	Sat	Sun
P. Mahan	7am-6pm	11am-12pm	●	off	off	●	●	●	off
L. Sands	8am-7pm	1pm-2pm	off	●	●	●	●	off	off
J. Manner	9am-8pm	2pm-3pm	●	●	off	off	●	●	off
M. Bayer	10am-9pm	3pm-4pm	off	off	●	●	off	●	●
S. Little	12am-11pm	5pm-6pm	●	●	●	●	off	off	off

8. Is this work schedule for one month, one year or one week?

Answer:

9. Do any two people on the list work the same exact schedule?

Answer:

10. Does L. Sands have to work on the weekend listed here?

Answer:

11. How many days a week does each person work?

Answer:

12. What time should J. Manner take his dinner break?

Answer:

13. Does M. Bayer have Sunday off?

Answer:

SK 7 Reading Work Schedules

A work schedule provides all the information an employee needs to know in order to be at work on the right day at the correct time. Work schedules are usually given out ahead of time to allow workers to plan and schedule events in their personal lives as well. It's a good idea to post your work schedule where it's easy to see and not likely to get lost. Many people attach it to the front of their refrigerators with a magnet, replacing it weekly or monthly with the latest one handed out.

It is very important to read your work schedule carefully, whether you are a new employee or have been with a company for years. Always make sure it is for the current week and not the week before or the week after. You get no extra points or pay if you show up for work at the right time but on the wrong day!

Work schedules are usually written and coordinated by company supervisors. Some supervisors allow employees to trade a work day as long as all shifts are covered; others do not. When beginning a new job, always check with your supervisor if you have any questions concerning your schedule or problems understanding it.

Work schedules are devised to help companies run smoothly and efficiently. The ability to read a work schedule correctly is a skill that helps make you a reliable and dependable employee— an asset to any company.

Quiz: SK7 - Reading Work Schedules

Name _____ Instructor's Initials _____
Date _____ Score _____
Competency Attained? Yes _____ No _____

Use the Teams List and Work Schedule below to answer the following questions:

TEAMS and SHIFTS

A Team:
9 a.m. - 5 p.m.

Scott Carter
Billy Depew
Randy McIntyre
Rod Langley
Pat Mahan
Courtney White
Brad Prince

B Team:
10 a.m. - 6 p.m.

Judy Frey
Reg Frey
Gene Ohlinger
Marilyn Murray
Ron Huebner
Karon Huebner

C Team:
11 a.m. - 7 p.m.

Polly Allison
Thomas Rhodes
Dan Ayars
Ron Wilson
Tom Scowden
Betty Scowden
Linda Yeargin
Ruth Ann Kujak

WORK SCHEDULE - JULY

SUN	MON	TUES	WED	THUR	FRI	SAT
1 B & C	2 C & A	3 C & A	4 A & B	5 A & B	6 B & C	7 B & C
8 C & A	9 C & A	10 A & B	11 A & B	12 B & C	13 B & C	14 C & A
15 C & A	16 A & B	17 A & B	18 B & C	19 B & C	20 C & A	21 C & A
22 A & B	23 A & B	24 B & C	25 B & C	26 C & A	27 C & A	28 A & B
29 A & B	30 B & C	31 B & C				

1. What hours does Scott Carter work during this month?
   a. 9 a.m. to 5 p.m.
   b. 11 a.m. to 7 p.m.

2. What hours does Tom Scowden work during this month?
   a. 9 a.m. to 5 p.m.
   b. 11 a.m. to 7 p.m.

3. Can Judy Frey make personal plans for Sunday, July 15th?
   a. Yes
   b. No

4. How many days will Pat Mahan work during the week of July 1-7?

    a. 4

    b. 5

5. How many days in a row does Brad Prince have to work during the week of July 8-14?

    a. 4

    b. 5

6. How many people are on Team A?

    a. 6

    b. 7

7. Is it OK for Billy Depew to switch days with Ron Wilson?

    a. Yes, as long as they promise to cover for each other.

    b. Not unless authorized.

8. Do all work schedules look alike?

    a. Yes

    b. No

9. Once you've read your schedule there's no need to keep it.

    a. True

    b. False

10. All scheduling is done monthly.

    a. True

    b. False

Working Basics

Reading Policy and Procedures Manuals

Basic Skills
Module SK 8

Congratulations! You've landed the job you were hoping to get. It's your first day at work and you've just been handed the company's "Policy and Procedures Manual." What do you do with it? You take it home and read it through from beginning to end. Then you go back through it and reread the sections that apply directly to you and your new job. If necessary, you read those sections again and again until you are sure you understand the policies and procedures of your new company.

Depending on the size of the company, a policy and procedure manual can be quite small (only a few pages) or very large (over a hundred pages). Most manuals contain a Table of Contents at the beginning. This is usually divided into two sections, one for company policies and the other for company procedures. A policy is a method of government or a course of conduct adopted by the company. A procedure is a particular course of action intended to achieve a result. The table of contents will list the different sections and specific topics under those sections. It will also give you the corresponding page numbers on which the information can be found. Among the topics covered in the **policy section** of such a manual are:

- Personnel forms
- Improper conduct on the job
- Attendance requirements
- Smoking
- Dress code
- Sexual harassment
- Telephone use

Among the areas covered in the **procedures section** of a manual are:

- Emergency procedures
- Safety Procedures
- Sick leave procedures
- Work scheduling
- Grievance procedures
- Employee termination
- Equipment maintenance

Many policy manuals also contain a list and description of the company's **benefits**, such as:

- Paid holidays
- Vacation
- Insurance
- Retirement (401-K plans)/pension plans
- Career opportunities

The key to reading a policy manual is to take your time and make sure you understand what is written. If after reading a certain section a few times, you still do not understand the policy or procedure exactly, check with your supervisor for details. For instance, when reading about the dress code policy for your new job, you may not be exactly sure what the company means by a "professional appearance." Does that mean business suits only, or are a pair of slacks and a dress shirt acceptable? If you are uncertain, ask your supervisor for more specific guidelines.

VIOLATING POLICIES AND PROCEDURES

Violations of company policies and procedures may result in such disciplinary action as:

- **Demotions:** Employees may be assigned to a lower level job and receive a cut in pay.

- **Suspensions:** Employees may receive mandatory leave without pay and/or benefits.

- **Immediate Termination:** Employees may lose their job and benefits.

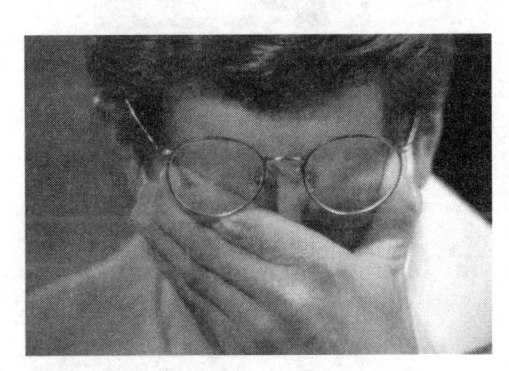

Companies keep records on all their employees in a personnel file. When it comes time to promote someone or to give someone a pay raise, employers will review the personnel files. It won't help your case if you have demotions, suspensions or warnings in your file.

You also want to avoid getting terminated from a job. This becomes a permanent mark on your record. Workers who have been dismissed often find it tough to find another job. The reason for this is because many times employers will call former employers to see how the person did on his/her prior job. Having a termination on your record creates a poor impression to the potential employer. It could prevent you from getting an interview or a job offer. In summary, when working, do all you can to keep a spotless record. Follow the rules and pay attention to all additions or changes to the policies and procedures at your workplace.

Working Basics

Reading your company's policy manual is a way to arm yourself with knowledge. This knowledge can make you an informed, aware employee, familiar with the ins and outs of the company's policies and procedures. Once you have read the manual, there can be no excuse for behavior outlined in the manual as unacceptable. "I didn't know" does not work because you are supposed to know - you should have read it in the policy and procedures manual you were given! So, carefully read and follow your company's policy manual and you are on your way to becoming an informed and knowledgeable employee. Informed and knowledgeable employees are quality employees — an asset to any company.

Quiz - SK 8: Reading Policy & Procedures Manuals

Name _____ Instructor's Initials _____
Date _____ Score _____
Competency Attained? Yes_____ No_____

Read the excerpt below from a company policy and procedures manual and answer the questions that follow:

> **3. Sick Leave** - Sick leave is a benefit/privilege provided by the company to its employees and should not be used for any other purpose than illness or injury. If the employee is not ill or injured then s/he is expected to be at work for regularly scheduled work periods. Sick leave may be used for doctor and/or dental appointments and will be charged to the exact or next greater quarter (.25) day.
> Immediately upon return to work, the employee must fill out a Leave Request Form and submit two copies to his/her supervisor. If leave is approved by a supervisor, both copies are then sent to the Director of Personnel. Failure to submit the Leave Request Form within one week of return will result in the absence being charged as unauthorized.
>
> **4. Emergency Leave** - Leave for compelling or emergency reasons may be approved on an individual basis based on evaluation of the circumstances. The employee must notify his or her supervisor of the circumstances at the earliest possible opportunity, and must fill out and submit two copies of the Leave Request to his or her supervisor and the Personnel Office within one week of returning to work.
>
> **5. Jury Duty Leave** - Upon receiving a summons for jury duty, the employee should notify his or her supervisor and the Personnel Office as soon as possible. Upon return to work from jury duty, the employee must submit two copies of the Leave Request Form.
>
> **6. Military Leave** - The employee should submit two copies of the Leave Request Form establishing necessary dates as soon as s/he is aware of the specific dates involved.
>
> **7. Personal Leave** - Personal leave requests should be submitted to the employee's supervisor and the Personnel Office with as much lead time as possible, or if notification cannot be made in advance then as soon as the employee returns to work.
>
> **Note:** All absences require the submission of a Leave Request Form. This includes quarter-day sick leave for scheduled doctor or dental appointments.

1. You may take a personal day off and use it as a sick leave day as long as you check with your supervisor first.

   a. True
   b. False

Working Basics

2. You have two weeks to submit a Sick Leave Request Form to your supervisor upon returning to work after an absence.

    a. True
    b. False

3. An Emergency Leave Request Form must first be submitted to the Director of Personnel, and then to your supervisor.

    a. True
    b. False

4. Leave for emergency reasons is approved on an individual basis.

    a. True
    b. False

5. If you are called for jury duty, you don't have to let your supervisor know until it's time for you to go.

    a. True
    b. False

6. Not all absences require the submission of a Leave Request Form.

    a. True
    b. False

7. It's important to give the company as much notice as possible when requesting any time off.

    a. True
    b. False

8. It's not all that important to read a policy manual if you're pretty sure of the company's rules.

    a. True
    b. False

9. Using the table of contents at the front of a manual is the fastest way to find where specific information is located.

    a. True
    b. False

10. If you don't understand something written in the manual, you should go directly to the company president for details.

    a. True
    b. False

Working Basics

Determining Sequential Events/Items

Basic Skills
Module SK 9

The old saying "first things first" sounds very simple but carries a great deal of truth. "Second things first" or "last things second" just doesn't work. Determining the correct order of events and items is a skill used often in daily life both on the job and at home. The word "sequential" is defined by Webster's dictionary as "relating to or arranged in a sequence." A "sequence" is defined as "a continuous or connected series." If you are trying to determine sequential events, your goal is to decide the order in which those events should occur. If you are trying to determine sequential items, your goal is to decide the order in which those items should be placed.

Determine the correct order of sequential events in the following morning-in-the-average-American-household scene:

___ eat breakfast

___ get dressed

___ turn off alarm clock

___ get out of bed

___ take a shower

___ pack a lunch

___ leave for work

It would be hard to pack a lunch after leaving for work, or to take a shower before getting out of bed!

Sequential items are easier to determine because they often are numbered. Therefore, determining sequential items is usually a matter of following the numbers correctly.

Working Basics

PRACTICE EXERCISE:

Your boss is out of town for the day and has left this memo:

```
MEMO

    First, type the letter to Mrs. Jones; have
Tom sign it for me; make three copies; give one
to Tom, put one on my desk and file the other
one; make sure the original is mailed today.
Next, call the home office and request extra
stationery and envelopes. Thanks.
```

In this case your boss has determined the sequential order of events. Would it matter if you changed the order, as long as you got it all done? Yes! It sure would! If you mail the letter before copying it you'll have some explaining to do when the boss returns.

What should you do after Tom signs the letter?

Answer:

Suppose you mailed the original letter and gave one to Tom. What should you do with the third and fourth copies?

Answer:

SK 9 Determining Sequential Events/Items

Sequential events and items often have key words that give clues about their order. For instance, first, second, third, fourth and fifth clearly show the first five items or steps in the order in which they are meant to occur. Another key phrase is the date or time of an event. Sequential events can be determined by the day or time they happened.

Other key words that indicate order are "next", "then," and "now." For instance, when determining the sequential order of events, "first" you look to see if the events are numbered, "next" you find out if they are dated, "then" you begin deciding their correct order and "now" you have enough information to determine their sequence.

Key Words That Indicate Order

First, Second, Third

Next

Then

Now

Directions of all types are usually given in sequential order. For example, the directions to assemble equipment or children's toys are given in sequential order. There are other times when you must determine the correct sequence of events.

When job hunting, for instance, you are the one who must decide the order of events such as these:

__complete resume	__read want ads
__send letters	__make follow up calls
__set appointments for interviews	__go to interviews
__celebrate new job	__accept position

© Copyright 1990-2003 The Paxen Group, Inc.

Working Basics

You can see how problems could crop up if you decide to celebrate the new job before going on the interview! For one thing, there would probably be no extra money to celebrate with!

FIRST THINGS FIRST

Determining the sequence of events and items is often a matter of common sense. Other times it's a matter of knowing and understanding dates and time. Sometimes it is simply a matter of reading carefully and following the given order of events or items. Whichever the case may be, when you are determining sequential events/items, listen to directions, read carefully, take your time and use your common sense. Remember, first things first!

Quiz: SK 9 - Determining Sequential Events/Items

Name _____ Instructor's Initials _____
Date _____ Score _____
Competency Attained? Yes____ No____

Put the events and items listed below in ascending order (from 1 - 3).
EXAMPLE:
_2_ Assemble bookcase
_1_ Gather tools needed for project
_3_ Put away tools and clean up

1.
　__ Get dressed
　__ Get out of bed
　__ Go to work

2.
　__ Turn on the copy machine
　__ Mail a copy of the letter
　__ Copy the letter

3.
　__ Step 2: Connect B to C
　__ Step 1: Connect A to B
　__ Step 3: Connect C to D

4.
　__ Sept. 2 - Depart for L.A.
　__ Sept. 6 - Depart L.A. for San Francisco
　__ Sept. 9 - Return home

5.
　__ 8:45 a.m.
　__ 8:15 a.m.
　__ 5:00 p.m.

6.
　__ Drive home
　__ Pick up child from sitter
　__ Leave work

7.
　__ No. 7
　__ No. 12
　__ No. 2

8.
　__ h
　__ j
　__ i

9.
　__ Twelfth
　__ Eleventh
　__ Tenth

10.
　__ Punch time clock
　__ Arrive at work
　__ Begin working

Working Basics

Reading Abbreviations

Basic Skills Module SK 12

It's very important to know and understand abbreviations. In our "hurry-up" world people are always abbreviating things. An abbreviation is a shortened version of a word used to save time or space. It often uses key letters that help you recognize the word. For example, the abbreviation *bldg.* uses the key letters b,l,d and g from the word *building*.

Abbreviations are used on signs, notices, advertisements, in written notes and letters. The ability to interpret these abbreviations may be critical to completing a task!

Each depositor insured to $100,000
FDIC
FEDERAL DEPOSIT INSURANCE CORPORATION

SEAL OF THE TENNESSEE VALLEY AUTHORITY
TVA
PROGRESS THROUGH RESOURCE DEVELOPMENT
1933

Ped.

dna
Defense Nuclear Agency

Here are some common abbreviations with their meanings:

Common Abbreviations

ASAP	As soon as possible
Ms.	a courtesy title used before a married or unmarried woman's last name
Mr.	a courtesy title used before a man's last name
Mrs.	a courtesy title used before a married woman's last name
a.m.	after 12:00 midnight and before 12:00 noon
p.m.	after 12:00 noon and before 12:00 midnight
P.E.	Physical Education
Rd.	Road
St.	Street
Pl.	Place
Blvd.	Boulevard
CIA	Central Intelligence Agency
Co.	Company
Dept.	Department

Think about your trip to training this morning. What abbreviations did you see on the way? What do they mean?

Abbreviation	Meaning

More Common Abbreviations

Inc.	Incorporated
FL	Florida
MA	Massachusetts
WA	Washington
DC	District of Columbia
IA	Iowa
TX	Texas
FBI	Federal Bureau of Investigation
EEO	Equal Employment Opportunity
i.e.	a Latin phrase meaning "that is"
e.g.	a Latin phrase meaning "for example"
c/o	in care of
ATTN.	attention
IRS	Internal Revenue Service
UN	United Nations
USA	United States of America

Working Basics

Look at this classified advertisement found in a local newspaper:

KITCHEN TBL.

Like new w/oak finish. One yr. old. Asking $200. Make offer. Call 728-3333 Ext. 123, 8AM - 6PM

What abbreviations are used and what do they mean?

Abbreviation	Meaning	Abbreviation	Meaning

When you are trying to figure out what an abbreviation stands for, it is almost like doing a puzzle. The only problem is you are missing some of the pieces. Look at the part of the word you have and try to figure which letters are missing. The other words in the sentence will often give you a clue about what the abbreviation means. For example, in the ad for the kitchen table above, you can tell that the abbreviation "Ext." has something to do with the telephone number. From there, you figure out which words have the letter Ext. that would make sense in this ad. Extension is the answer. It's really not too hard.

Notice that we used the word *ad* as an abbreviation for the word *advertisement*. This is a common abbreviation understood by most people.

Working Basics

List as many abbreviations and their meanings as you can think of on the chart below.

Abbreviation	Meaning	Abbreviation	Meaning

There are many more abbreviations than the ones on your list. Also remember many companies, groups, or organizations will use their own abbreviations with their own meanings.

SK 12 Reading Abbreviations

PRACTICE EXERCISE:

Now practice to see how well you can read abbreviations. Read the following memo and set of directions. List the meaning of the numbered abbreviations in the spaces provided.

---

(1) **MEMO**

To: All Employees

(2) Fr: John Smith

(3) RE: Social Events Suggestions

Date: January 8th

The (4) chmn. of the social committee has asked that each person spend at least one half (5) hr. thinking of ideas for the (6) corp. Christmas Party, annual cook-out, (7) etc. Your ideas will be accepted (8) @ the next (9) wkly. staff meeting.

Also, all employees are asked to obey the new posted speed limit of 25 (10) m.p.h.

---

1. _____   6. _____

2. _____   7. _____

3. _____   8. _____

4. _____   9. _____

5. _____   10. _____

Working Basics

Quiz - SK 12: Reading Abbreviations

Name _____ Instructor's Initials _____
Date _____ Score _____
Competency Attained? Yes_____ No_____

Write the full word or phrase for each italicized abbreviation in the space below.

IN CASE OF FIRE:

(1)*1st* Floor (2)*Emps*:

  -Exit (3)*@* the (4)*S.* end of the (5)*bldg.*

2nd Floor Emps:

  -Exit @ the (6)*N.* end of bldg.

Basement Level Emps:

  -Exit @ the center door, go (7)*↑* the (8)*lt.* side stairs and out the (9)*E.* exit on 1st floor.

IMPORTANT! DO NOT USE THE (10)*ELEV.*

1. _____ 6. _____

2. _____ 7. _____

3. _____ 8. _____

4. _____ 9. _____

5. _____ 10. _____

continued on next page

Working Basics

Read the following ad, then write the full word or phrase for each abbreviation in the space below.

NURSES WANTED!

All shifts. [11]*P/T* or [12]*FT*. [13]*Exp.* [14]*req.* Salary $28/hr. [15]*w/*great benefits. Apply in person [16]*Thurs.* -[17]*Sat.* 10:00 am-4:00 p.m. Bring [18]*res.* and [19]*refs.*

Sand Lake [20]*Med.* Center, Hwy. 441, Sandalwood.

11. _____
12. _____
13. _____
14. _____
15. _____
16. _____
17. _____
18. _____
19. _____
20. _____

Working Basics

Reading Safety Warnings

Basic Skills
Module SK 15

Safety warnings come in all shapes and sizes, and can be found in many different places. Their purpose is to warn you about something that might hurt you or damage equipment. Signs like **CAUTION: WET FLOOR** are to warn you that the floor is wet—be careful not to slip and fall. Safety warnings are not intended to spoil your fun. They are for your own safety. Hundreds of accidents happen because people have not bothered to read safety warnings.

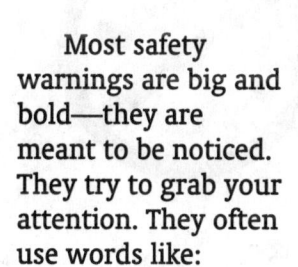

Most safety warnings are big and bold—they are meant to be noticed. They try to grab your attention. They often use words like:

- WARNING
- DANGER
- CAUTION
- NOTICE
- SHARP
- POISON

DANGER CONSTRUCTION AREA

WARNING

CAUTION FLAMMABLE LIQUIDS

NOTICE THESE DOORS MUST BE KEPT CLOSED

Working Basics

The Federal Occupational Safety and Health Act regulates safety labels as follows:

- **DANGER** is used to indicate a hazardous situation which has a high chance of death or severe injury.
- **WARNING** is used to indicate a hazardous situation which has some chance of death or serious injury.
- **CAUTION** is used to indicate a hazardous situation which may result in a minor or moderate injury.
- **NOTICE** is used to indicate a statement of company policy as the message relates directly or indirectly to the safety of personnel or property.
- **GENERAL SAFETY** signs indicate general instructions about safe work practices and reminders of proper procedures.

Safety warnings often use graphic symbols or pictures to illustrate their meanings. For example, a lightening bolt is used to show electricity or high voltage. A cigarette with a cross through it is used to show that no smoking is permitted. Using a graphic picture helps people to easily see what the safety warning means. This way, even someone who cannot read or who doesn't know the language would know what the sign means.

Here are some examples of the wide variety of safety warnings:

- The sign at the gas station pump that says **TURN IGNITION OFF WHILE PUMPING GAS.**
- The label that says **KEEP AWAY FROM CHILDREN.** The contents probably are poisonous.
- A sign reading **HIGH VOLTAGE-DO NOT TOUCH.** A large dose of electricity can kill a person.
- **WEAR SAFETY GLASSES** warns you that particles, sparks, etc. are in the area and might damage your eyes.
- The label on a radio may tell you not to turn it on near the bathtub or any other water into which it might fall. Electricity travels very quickly and easily through water, and you could be killed.

SK 15 Reading Safety Warnings

Brainstorm a moment and think of as many safety warnings as you can. Write or draw them in the space below.

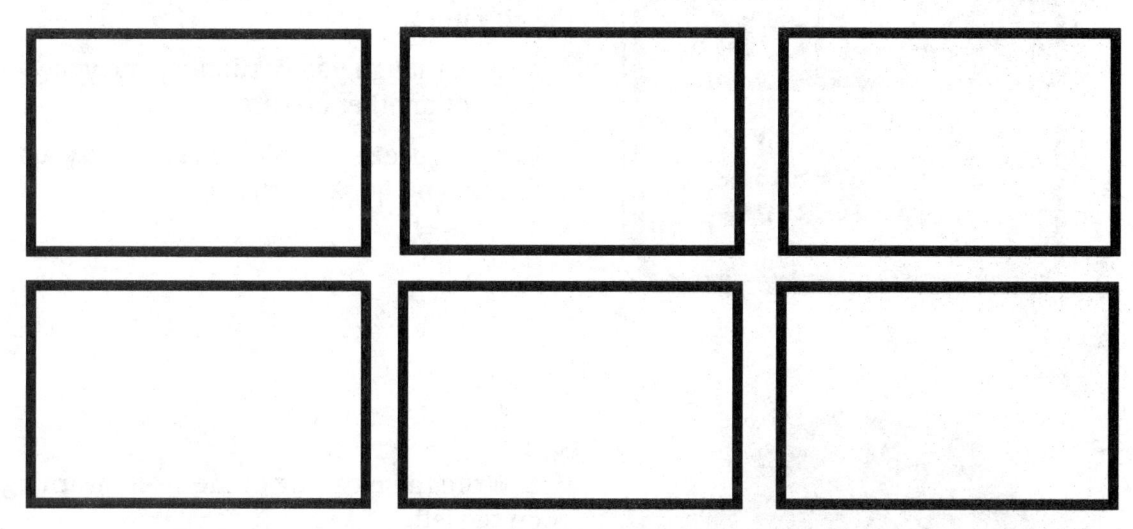

Read the safety warnings below and decide which action (a or b) you should take.

DANGER

ROTATING BLADE. DO NOT PUT HANDS OR FEET UNDER THE MOWER WHEN ENGINE IS RUNNING.

1. Something is caught in your lawn mower.

   a. You immediately feel under the mower with your hand.

   b. You turn off the mower and then check underneath.

Working Basics

CAUTION

WEIGHT CAPACITY 750 LBS. OR FIVE PERSONS. DO NOT OVERLOAD

2. You approach the elevator and see the sign on the left. You see six large men already in the elevator.

   a. Even though you're running late you wait for another elevator.

   b. You squeeze in beside them, cross your fingers and hope for the best.

3.

   a. Write the meaning of the safety warning on the left.

   _____
   _____

   b. What might happen if you do not follow the safety warning?

   _____
   _____

CAUTION

MEN WORKING ABOVE

4.

   a. Write the meaning of the safety warning on the left.

   _____
   _____

   b. What might happen if you do not follow the safety warning?

   _____
   _____

DANGER
NO SMOKING, MATCHES OR OPEN LIGHTS

5.
   a. Write the meaning of the safety warning on the left.

   _____

   _____

   b. What might happen if you do not follow the safety warning?

   _____

   _____

Working Basics

Quiz: SK 15 - Reading Safety Warnings

Name _____ Instructor's Initials _____
Date _____ Score _____
Competency Attained? Yes_____ No_____

Read each warning below and select the letter of the matching description.

___1. WARNING! DO NOT OPERATE MOWER WITHOUT GRASS BAG ATTACHED.

___2. EXIT HERE IN CASE OF FIRE

___3. KEEP OUT OF DIRECT SUNLIGHT

___4. WATCH YOUR STEP

___5. CAUTION: IF YOU ARE PREGNANT OR NURSING A BABY, SEE YOUR DOCTOR BEFORE USING THIS PRODUCT

___6. BEWARE OF DOG

___7. DANGER! HARMFUL IF SWALLOWED

___8. DANGER—AUTHORIZED PERSONNEL ONLY

___9. TURN MOTOR OFF BEFORE REPAIRING

___10. DO NOT TOUCH

a. This product will become dangerous if it is heated. Keep in a dark place away from light and heat.

b. Make sure the grass bag is attached to your mower before you mow the lawn.

c. This product could harm your child or unborn baby. Ask your doctor if it is safe for you to use this product.

d. If you are in a building and you hear the fire alarm, go to this door to get out.

e. Be careful, the floor is wet or slippery, or there is a step up or down ahead.

f. You should not be here, unless your supervisor has OK'D it.

g. Rover is not a nice dog, and he might bite you if you trespass on his territory.

h. Don't eat or drink this product, and keep it away from children who might.

i. Don't try to fix this machine while the motor is running. You might get hurt or break the machine.

j. This might be dangerous to you for some hidden or unknown reason. Keep your hands off!

© Copyright 1990-2003 The Paxen Group, Inc.

Working Basics

SK 16 Reading Procedures

Working Basics

Reading Procedures

Basic Skills
Module SK 16

You've just bought a VCR, and you can't wait to tape that great show at 3:00 a.m. But first you have to learn how to program its memory. All those buttons, knobs and digital numbers...it will take Albert Einstein himself to figure this out!

This is a good example of how important it is to be able to read procedure manuals and owner's manuals. These manuals tell you all about a product, safety tips, usage instructions, how to take care of it and what to do if something goes wrong.

Owner's manuals and procedure manuals often contain information about warranties and guarantees. It is important to keep these manuals. You might need to refer to them in the future. If the manuals contain repair instructions, you should keep them in case the products break down.

If you have a job in a paint store, a customer might ask you, *"Can you match the paint to this color?"*

© Copyright 1990-2003 The Paxen Group, Inc.

Working Basics

If you're not familiar with the product, don't panic. Just remember these steps:

INSTRUCTIONS FOR READING PROCEDURES

- Look in the procedure manual at the table of contents. You will see section headings like *Safety Practices*, *Equipment Maintenance*, and *Operating Instructions*.
- Find the right section and there you will find the answer.
- Look in the glossary for terms you don't understand.
- Sometimes manuals have color coded sections—check the guide/legend for the matching color and information.
- Some manuals have an alphabetical index which will help you to find a specific problem or process faster. Check at the back of the book for an index.

PRACTICE EXERCISE:

Look at this table of contents taken from a manual for a gas-powered hedger.

On what page(s) will you find the answers to these questions?

1. How do you sharpen the blade? _____

2. How often should you change the oil? _____

3. How do you start the hedger? _____

4. What is the easiest way to hold it? _____

5. What fuel type should be used? _____

TABLE OF CONTENTS	
Introduction	3
Safety Rules	5
Unpacking the Hedger	6
Assembling the Hedger	7
Fuel and Oil	8
Starting the Hedger	9
Normal Operation	9
Cold Weather Operation	10
Storage of the Hedger	11
Maintenance and Repair	13
Troubleshooting	16
If You Need Help	20

Now read the following excerpt from a procedures manual and answer the questions which follow.

EXPO Computer Microprocessor Operating Instructions

GENERAL TROUBLESHOOTING CHECKLIST

Before proceeding with the list of symptoms and solutions in this chapter, review the following checklist. Trouble with your system may result from a problem as simple as a faulty connection. Run through the following steps first.

Check Connections:

Check the system connections in this manner:

1. Turn off the system unit.

2. Unplug the system unit from the wall.

3. Remove and reinstall the keyboard cable. (See Chapter 3)

4. Remove and reinstall the two monitor cables. (See Chapter 3)

5. Remove and reinstall the power cable from the system unit. (See Chapter 3)

Check the Power:

Then check the power in the following manner:

1. Plug a working appliance such as a lamp into the wall outlets used for the system unit. Check to be sure the outlet has power and is working correctly.

2. Plug the system unit and monitor into the same working wall outlets.

3. Turn on the monitor.

4. Turn on the system unit.

If after completing the steps, you still have no power to your system, turn to "Preparing the Personal Computer for Servicing" in Chapter 7.

1. What should you do if you need more information about removing and installing the keyboard cable?

_____
_____

2. When checking connections, what should you do after turning off the system unit?

_____
_____

3. What's the first step in checking the power?

_____
_____

4. After checking the connections and power, you still have no power to your computer system. What is the next step?

_____
_____

5. If you plug a lamp into the same outlet your computer was plugged into and find it doesn't work, what does this tell you?

_____
_____

Keep one final thing in mind when following procedure manuals: the procedures are there for a reason. To have the fewest problems, safest operation and least time for repairs, follow the manual and do the steps correctly.

Quiz: SK 16 - Reading Procedures

Name _____ Instructor's Initials _____
Date _____ Score _____
Competency Attained? Yes_____ No_____

Look at this table of contents. On what pages will you most likely find the answers to the following questions?

E-Z CLEAN VACUUM

Assembling the Vacuum Cleaner	5-7
Cleaner Description and Unpacking	3,4
Energy Saving Tips	20
How to Use	
Cleaning Tools	10-13
Special Features	9
Upright Cleaner	7-10
If You Have a Problem	19
Important Safeguards	2
Lubrication	20
Maintenance	
Authorized Service	19
Replacing Belt	15-17
Replacing Brushes	17-18
Replacing Headlight	15
Replacing Throw Away Bag	14

---

1. How do you use the tools that came with the vacuum cleaner? _____

2. The cleaner is jammed. Where can you find how to fix it? _____

3. If you find that you can't fix it, where can you get the machine fixed? _____

Working Basics

4. How do you change the bag when it gets full? _____
5. You've just received your new vacuum cleaner. What is the best way to unpack it? _____
6. Are there safety precautions you should take when using the vacuum? _____
7. How do you replace the belt? _____
8. You've unpacked the new vacuum. How do you put it together? _____
9. Is there a description of the vacuum's parts? _____
10. What special cleaning features does this vacuum have? _____

Working Basics

Understanding Symbols

Basic Skills
Module SK 20

Do you know that you are surrounded by symbols? You are so used to them that you probably don't realize you're seeing them. Below are some examples of symbols that should be familiar to you.

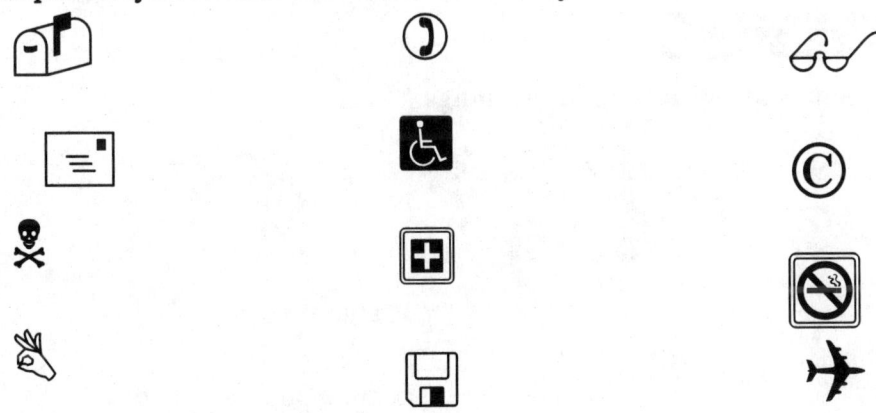

A symbol is a "little picture" that represents a phrase or an idea that would normally take several more words to explain it. They are shortcuts that take up less space and are instantly recognizable—you know right away what they mean. For example, look at the two doors below.

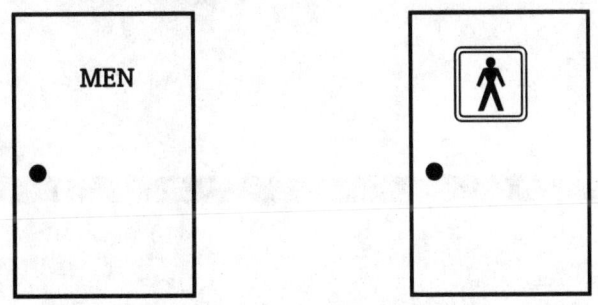

Which one would you recognize more quickly? Which one would a person who did

Working Basics

not speak English recognize more quickly? Which one would a child or a person who could not read recognize more quickly?

Symbols have the added plus that people of all nations and languages can understand them. People who cannot read can understand them. Symbols certainly make life easier.

To understand what a symbol means, look at the symbol and ask yourself, "What is this a picture of?" Then translate the symbol into words. For example, if you are at the gas station and see a sign that has a picture of a cigarette with a slash through it, the sign means, *No Smoking.* A dollar sign ($) means *money.* Get the idea? See how well you understand some common symbols by completing the practice exercises below.

PRACTICE EXERCISE:

Match the symbols below with their meanings.

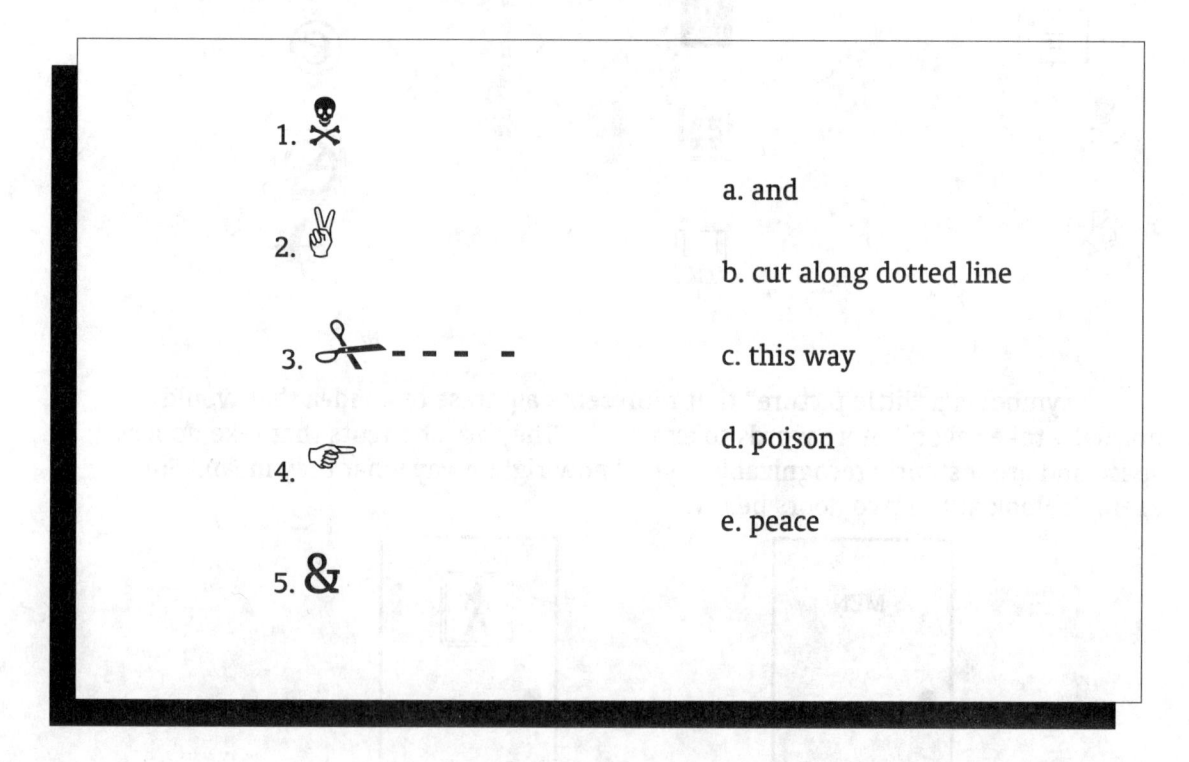

1. ☠

2. ✌

3. ✂ - - - -

4. ☞

5. &

a. and

b. cut along dotted line

c. this way

d. poison

e. peace

SK 20 Understanding Symbols

Can you think of any other symbols you have seen? Draw them in the boxes below and write the meaning of each symbol next to it.

Try reading this sentence:

✝ & ✝ want ✌ & ♥ in the 🇺🇸

Write its meaning below:

_____
_____

Quiz: SK 20 - Understanding Symbols

Name _____ Instructor's Initials _____
Date _____ Score _____
Competency Attained? Yes_____ No_____

Match the following symbols with their meanings. Write the correct letter of each symbol in the blank next to its meaning.

a. ↑

b. !

c. ✂ - - - - -

d. @

e. #

f. %

g. $

h. 🚭

i. (person in chair)

j. 🚫🐕

k. ♀ (child figure)

l. ♿

m. (stairs)

n. DANGER CONSTRUCTION AREA

o. ♂

___1. no smoking
___2. up
___3. stairs
___4. male
___5. dollar
___6. at
___7. number
___8. percent
___9. handicapped
___10. baby
___11. danger
___12. cut on the dotted line
___13. woman
___14. no dogs
___15. exclamation point

Working Basics

Alphabetizing

Basic Skills
Module SK 21

There are so many instances in daily life and at work where alphabetizing is important. Inventories (the number of items) of stock, supplies, files and even work stations are often put in alphabetical order. Daily, you are faced with finding products in stores by alphabetizing. Finding information, in a phone book for example, is often done by alphabetizing. Even recipes in a cookbook are alphabetized.

Because so much of what we use every day is arranged in alphabetical order, it is necessary for you to develop this skill.

Alphabetize means to arrange items in a specific order, based on the first letters of the item from A - Z. Always use the first letter in the word you are going to alphabetize. If you have two words with the same first letter, go to the next letter to the right and compare them. Which comes first in the alphabet? Then place that word before the other.

b<u>a</u>nd

br<u>o</u>wn

"a" comes before "r" so "band" goes before "brown"

Working Basics

This also works if you have two letters that are the same, or three letters, and so on.

fir

fire

firearm

fireplace

Notice above that some of these words had the exact same letters, up to a point. **Fir** and **fire**. **Fir** comes first because it has less letters than **fire**.

List six items found in the room around you.

Now put them in alphabetical order. Use the alphabet below as a guide, if you need it.

A B C D E F G H I J K L M N O P Q R S T U V W X Y Z

54

SK 21 Alphabetizing

PRACTICE EXERCISES:

Put the names below into alphabetical order by last name from 1-8. Place a 1 by the name which would come first, a 2 by the next one, and so on.

___ Jones, Allen

___ Smith, Jane W.

___ Hunt, George

___ Johnson, Earl

___ Rogers, William F.

___ Mann, Barbara T.

___ Bernard, John

___ Smith, Jennifer A.

Now look at a dictionary. A dictionary has **guide words** at the top of the page that help you find the words which fall between those **guide words**.

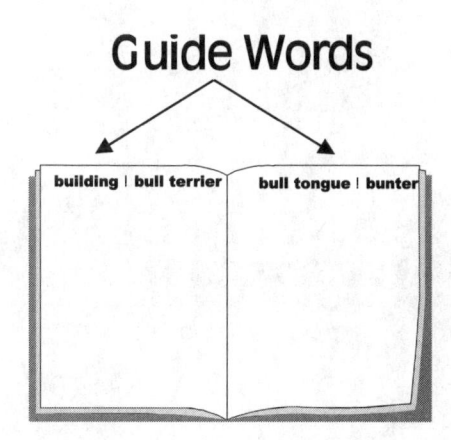

Guide Words

building | bull terrier   bull tongue | bunter

Working Basics

For example, if **germ** and **give** are the guide words, which of the words below will be found on that page? Circle them.

    get

    green

    ghost

    gang

    girl

    glove

Remember, the key to alphabetizing is knowing the order of the alphabet. Look at the first letter of each word and move to the right as needed to put the words in order. From the library, to home, to work, you need to know how to alphabetize to function well in all of these places.

Quiz - SK 21 Alphabetizing

Name _____ Instructor's Initials _____
Date _____ Score _____
Competency Attained? Yes_____ No_____

Here is a list of guide words and a set of unalphabetized words. Match the words to the appropriate set of guide words. Place your answer in the spaces provided. If none match, write "none."

Guide Words			Unalphabetized Words
_____ 1. nightshirt	-	nuance	A. distrust
_____ 2. grasshopper	-	guardian	B. and
_____ 3. preview	-	project	C. web
_____ 4. add	-	age	D. task
_____ 5. alongside	-	animate	E. north
_____ 6. zen	-	zucchini	F. slate
_____ 7. scoop	-	seize	G. score
_____ 8. context	-	creep	H. infect
_____ 9. waft	-	weight	I. zoo
_____ 10. plastics	-	pollen	J. crazy
_____ 11. bracket	-	brow	K. lesson
_____ 12. tamper	-	tend	L. brick
_____ 13. discredit	-	divine	M. print
_____ 14. left	-	limp	N. addict
_____ 15. indirect	-	instant	O. sin
_____ 16. bellow	-	bit	P. bird
_____ 17. shrewd	-	skillet	Q. grave
_____ 18. ebony	-	ember	R. knit
_____ 19. kickback	-	lamb	S. eleven
_____ 20. various	-	vile	T. way

Working Basics

21. You are looking in the phone book for your friend Steve Adams' phone number. Will it be on the page with these guide words? **Abdul - Abrams**?

    a. Yes

    b. No

22. Your boss has asked you to file Mrs. Waters' folder alphabetically by last name in the file cabinet. **After** which of these names does the folder go?

    a. Webster

    b. Wasicki

    c. Wolman

    d. White

23. You are trying to find Juniper Street in the index on a map. Where will it be listed?

    a. after Mangrove Street

    b. between Rose Drive and South Street

    c. before First Avenue

    d. between Grant Street and Lilac Lane

24. You are looking for a recipe in the index of a cookbook. You would like to have "Chicken Supreme" for dinner tonight. Where will "Chicken Supreme" be listed?

    a. between Cream Puffs and Cobbler

    b. after Chocolate Layer Cake

    c. before Chutney

    d. before Cheddar Cheese Soup

25. The supply room at your company is arranged in alphabetical order. You have just run out of paper clips. Where will you find them?

    a. after rubber bands

    b. between paper bags and scissors

    c. between erasers and felt tip markers

    d. before message pads

Working Basics

Finding Pages

Basic Skills
Module SK 22

The trick to finding pages is finding where the page numbers are located on the page. Some books print the page numbers in the middle of the bottom of the page. Others number the page on the right or left side at the bottom of the page. Others put the page numbers at the top of the page. While the location of page numbers varies from book to book, one thing is always the same:

Pages are numbered in order from the lowest number up to the highest number.

If you know the page number you need to find, you can "thumb" through the pages until you find it. Since the numbers are in order, this is easy. If you need to find page 48 and you open the book to page 56, what would you do?

You should turn back 8 pages.

Using Tables of Contents

If you need to look up a page and all you have to go by is a title, word or subject, how do you find the page? You could just thumb through the book until you find the topic you wanted but there is an easier and faster way- using the table of contents.

If the book has a table of contents, it will be in the front of the book. It lists the sections or chapters of the book and the page numbers where they are located. First, find the chapter or section your topic is under, and run your finger across to the right for the correct page number. You should be able to find the topic on that page or after it. Some tables of contents have subheadings under each section or chapter. This makes finding a subject even quicker and easier.

Here is a sample table of contents:

Table of Contents	Page No.
EMPLOYMENT FORMS	1
Job Application	2
Employment Contract	4
W-4 Form	5
FIGURING OUT WAGES	7
USING A CHECKING ACCOUNT	8
Deposits	8
Checks	10
Check Register	13
LOANS	17
Security	17
Payments	19
Loan Types	21
Interest on Loans	23

On what page would you find types of loans? _____

On what page would you find a job application form? _____

Tables of contents can be organized in different ways. Some examples include the use of:

- Roman numbers
- Arabic numbers
- Tabs (indentions)
- Geographical sections
- Alphabetically
- Systematically

and there are others. The example below is organized by Roman numbers. Look at the table of numbers on the next page to familiarize yourself with Roman numbers and Arabic numbers. Then complete the practice exercise.

Sample Table of Contents - Roman Numbers

CONTENTS

Author's Note	xi
Forward	xix
BOOK I: This Side of the "Smoking Gun"	1
BOOK II: The Haldeman Approach	43
BOOK III: The War - and the Wires	77
BOOK IV: Who Ordered the Break-in?	119
BOOK V: The Hidden Story of Watergate	165
BOOK VI: The Real Story of the Tapes	169
BOOK VII: The Mysteries of the Cover-Up	213
BOOK VIII: The Beginning of the End	253
BOOK IX: Personal Diary of the Final Days	297

Working Basics

Table of Numbers:		Arabic	Roman	Arabic	Roman
Arabic	Roman	6	VI	12	XII
1	I	7	VII	13	XIII
2	II	8	VIII	14	XIV
3	III	9	IX	15	XV
4	IV	10	X	50	L
5	V	11	XI	100	C

DIRECTIONS: Write each Arabic number in Roman numeral form.

_____ a. 6

_____ b. 10

_____ c. 51

_____ d. 9

_____ e. 12

_____ f. 15

Using Indexes

Another place to look up page numbers is the index. Indexes are found at the back of a book. An index is a good place to look if the table of contents is too general to help you. It lists key words, topics and names, and the page or pages where they can be found. These subjects are listed in alphabetical order. Here is a sample index:

Index

Address labels, 135, 139
Audience, 8
Bond paper, 130, 131
Budget, see Costs
Camera, selection of, 81
Carton, of paper, 133
Cartoonists
Color,
   in design, 92, 93, 96
   photographs, 111
Costs,
   paper, 129, 133

If you cannot find the topic you need, look under similar headings. In the index above, if you look up **Budget**, the index instructs you to look under **Costs** instead.

On what page(s) would you find information about the cost of paper? _____

On what page(s) would you find information about color photographs? _____

In school, at home and at work, you'll always come across times when you need to look up something in a reference book. Use the indexes and tables of contents to help you find the pages quickly.

Working Basics

Quiz - SK 22: Finding Pages

Name _____ Instructor's Initials _____
Date _____ Score _____
Competency Attained? Yes____ No____

Directions: Using the table of contents below, find the correct page number for each item.

Table of Contents	Page No.
SECTION I	1
Welcome to Oceanside	2
Training Course Objectives	3
Training Schedule	4
Benefits and Policies	5
Wages	16
SECTION II	17
Wait staff	18
Job Descriptions	19
Setting the Table	21
Opening/Closing Responsibilities	3
Dealing with Guests	26
Taking an Order	28
Checks and Balances	30
Wait staff Schedule	32
Safety	36

1. On what page will you find the benefits and policies? _____
2. On what page will you find how to take an order? _____
3. On what page will you find the training schedule? _____
4. On what page will you find how to set the table? _____
5. On what page will you find the training course objectives? _____
6. On what page will you find information about paychecks? _____
7. On what page will you find the company policy for sick leave? _____
8. If your boss asked you to turn to page 4, what topic will you be looking up? _____
9. What topic is found on page 36? _____
10. On what page will you find safety procedures? _____

Working Basics

DIRECTIONS: Using the index on the right, find the correct page number which answers the question.

11. On what page will you find the organizational chart? _____

12. On what page will you find how to balance a cash drawer? _____

13. On what page will you find safety procedures? _____

14. On what page will you find closing procedures? _____

15. On what page will you find information about a cook's helper? _____

16. On what page will you find information about cleaning a uniform? _____

17. On what page will you find out about wages? _____

18. Your boss asks you to locate a kitchen utensil. You don't know what it looks like. On what page will you find out about this utensil? _____

19. Suppose you are a waiter and are asked to set the tables in the dining room. You are having trouble remembering where the small fork should go. On what page will you find this information? _____

20. On what page will you find the job description for a cashier? _____

INDEX

Balancing a cash drawer, 45
Benefits, 6
Closing procedures, 24
Credit purchases, 19
Guest information, 50
Job descriptions,
   cashier, 7
   cook, 8
   cook's helper, 9
   Wait staff, 10
   organization chart, 11
Opening procedures, 25
Orders, 14
Organizational chart, *see Job Descriptions*
Policies. 5
Safety procedures, 17
Schedule, 20
Setting tables, 40
Uniforms,
   cleaning, 32
   purchasing, 33
Utensils, 37
Wages, 3

Working Basics

Adding Whole Numbers

Basic Skills
Module SK 30

In your daily life and on the job, the ability to add whole numbers is essential. This module contains basic rules for adding.

Whole Numbers

A **whole number** is a complete number, with no parts missing. For example:

0 1 2 3 4 5 6 7 8 9 10

These are whole numbers. They can be combined to make larger whole numbers. 23 is a whole number. So is 1,350,987. There are other numbers such as ½, 3/4 and 5/8 which are not whole numbers. These numbers are called fractions, because they are only a "fraction" or part of a whole number. In this module you will only be adding whole numbers.

Addition is "putting together" or adding two or more numbers to find the **sum,** or answer. When you see the plus symbol (+), this means to add. Put 3 lemons and 3 lemons together and what do you get? The answer is 6 lemons. When adding numbers, the answer goes after the equal sign (=), as in this example:

3 lemons + 3 lemons = 6 lemons

Working Basics

When you add numbers, you can add them going across, as in the example above, or you can add them in a column:

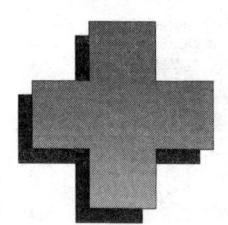

```
  3
+ 3
  6
```

Place Value

A number can be any size, such as   5   50   567   34,678   or larger.

- A number is made up of one or more digits.
- A single number like two (2) has only one digit.
- The number twenty-two (22) has two digits.

How many digits are in the number seven-hundred sixty-three?	Write your answer here.

Each digit of a number has a **place value.** The place value of a digit is shown by where it is in the number. For example, in the number 1234, 1 has the place value of thousands, 2 is in the hundreds place, 3 is in the tens place, and 4 is in the ones place.

Example:

Billions	Millions	Thousands	Hundreds
1,	2 5 0,	0 0 0,	0 0 0

This number is written: 1,250,000,000. When you read this number you say, "One billion, two-hundred-fifty million."

68

SK 30 Adding Whole Numbers

Here is a review.

Look at this **ONE-DIGIT** number   6

The number, 6, has only one digit, or one place value, and means six ones.

Look at this **TWO-DIGIT** number   18

The number, 18, has two digits and two place values. There is a 8 in the ones place and a 1 in the tens place. This means you have 8 ones and 1 ten which equals 18.

Look at the **THREE-DIGIT** number   346

The number 346 has three digits and three place values. There is a 6 in the ones place, a 4 in the tens place and a 3 in the hundreds place. 6 ones and 4 tens and 3 hundreds make the number 346.

For each of the numbers below, write how many ones, tens, hundreds or thousands it has. The first one is done for you.

Number	Thousands	Hundreds	Tens	Ones
455		4	5	5
982				
34				
761				
1,999				
6,631				

Working Basics

When you are adding numbers with more than one digit, start by working from the right— adding all the digits in the ones place. Then move left to add the digits in the tens place, hundreds place and so on. Example:

Hundreds	Tens	Ones
2	3	1
3	4	0
+ 2	0	0
7	7	1

STEP 1: Add the numbers in the ones column: **1+0+0=1**

STEP 2: Add the numbers in the tens column: **3+4+0=7**

STEP 3: Add the numbers in the hundreds column: **2+3+2=7**

ANSWER: 771

Adding Numbers

If you add 4 and 6, what do you get?

$$\begin{array}{r} 4 \\ + \ 6 \\ \hline 10 \end{array}$$

When adding, you must **carry over** any digits that are higher than 9 to the next place. In the example, the "1" is carried over into the tens place and the "0" remains in the ones place.

Examples:

1. Add 29 and 21 and what do you get?

```
  Tens  Ones
   2⁺¹    9      So write         29
  + 2    1                      + 21
    5   ⑩                        50
```

SK 30 Adding Whole Numbers

STEP ONE: Add the numbers in the ones column: 9+1=10. Leave the 0 in the ones place and carry the 1 over to the tens place.

STEP TWO: Add the numbers in the tens column. Don't forget to add the 1 you carried over from step one. 1+2+2=5

ANSWER: 50

2. Add 905 and 106 and what do you get?

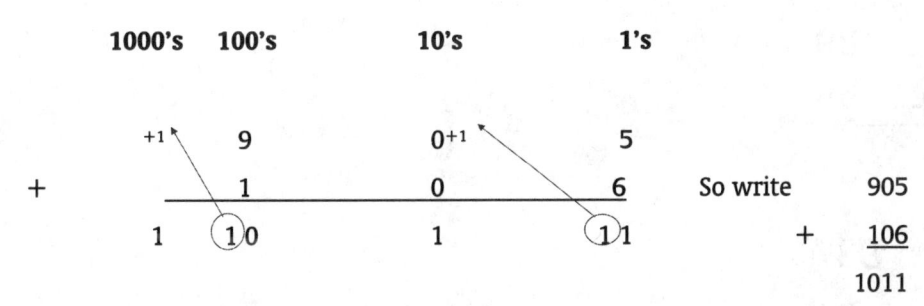

1000's	100's	10's	1's
	$^{+1}$ 9	0^{+1}	5
+	1	0	6
1	(1)0	1	(1)1

So write
$$\begin{array}{r} 905 \\ +\ 106 \\ \hline 1011 \end{array}$$

STEP ONE: Add the numbers in the ones column: **5+6 = 11**. Leave the 1 in the ones place and carry 1 over to the tens place.

STEP TWO: Add the numbers in the tens column. Don't forget to add the 1 you carried over from step one. **0+0+1=1.**

STEP THREE: Add the numbers in the hundreds column: **9+1 = 10**. Carry the 1 over to the thousands column.

STEP FOUR: Add the numbers in the thousands column: 1+0+0=1

ANSWER: 1011

When you add numbers, **always** check your answers carefully.

Working Basics

PRACTICE EXERCISES:

1.   100
         12
    +   13

2.   1000
    + 989

3.   89
    + 23

4.   937
    +   31

5.   56
    + 39

6. In the number 2,399, which number is in the hundreds place?
   a. 9
   b. 2
   c. 3

7. In the number 569,105, which number is in the tens place?
   a. 5
   b. 0
   c. 1

SK 30 Adding Whole Numbers

8. You collect tickets at a movie theater. If you collected 47 tickets on Monday, 80 tickets on Tuesday, and 37 tickets on Wednesday, how many tickets total did you collect for those three days?

9. You need to order supplies for the office. Mark needs 10 pens and 4 notepads. Sandy needs 6 pens and 3 notepads. Jack needs 21 pens and 8 notepads. How many total notepads and pens do you need to order?

10. If you are 27 years old, how old will you be in 16 years?

How did you do? If you missed any problems, go back and review the rules of addition.

Working Basics

Quiz: SK 30 - Adding Whole Numbers

Name _____ Instructor's Initials _____
Date _____ Score _____
Competency Attained?   Yes _____   No _____

Directions: Add the following whole numbers.

1.   92
      + 45
      ———

2.   890
      + 24
      ———

3.   245
      + 19
      ———

4.   36
      + 61
      ———

5.   95
      + 15
      ———

6.   77
      + 52
      ———

7.   13
      + 8
      ———

8.   30
      + 18
      ———

9. You work in a factory. On Monday you assembled 26 tables. On Tuesday you assembled 43 tables. On Wednesday you assembled 19 tables. How many total tables did you assemble for Monday, Tuesday and Wednesday?

continued next page

Working Basics

10. Your boss asked you to order fertilizer for all the supervisors. Jerry needs 40 pounds of fertilizer. Tony needs 23 pounds. Susan needs 35 pounds. How many total pounds of fertilizer do you need to order?

Subtracting Whole Numbers

Basic Skills
Module SK 31

There are very few jobs that do not involve the use of subtraction in one form or another. From bank tellers to inventory clerks to engineers, subtracting whole numbers plays a big part in day-to-day work operations.

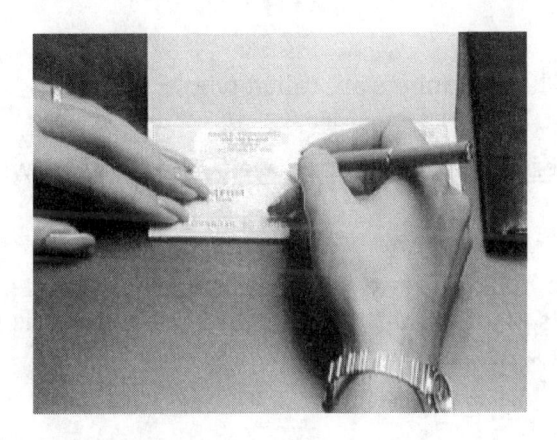

These skills are also used at home. How many times per day do you find yourself using subtraction just around the house? Whether you are calculating daily expenses or balancing your checkbook, you often use these skills without even being aware of them.

Stop and think for a moment.

List three activities you did today that used subtraction:
1.
2.
3.

Working Basics

Place Values

As with addition, a number can be any size such as 4, 40, 400, 40,000 or even higher.

Each digit represents a value. The place value of the digit is shown by where it is in the number. For example, in the number 4567, 4 has the place value of thousands, 5 is in the hundreds place, 6 is in the tens place and 7 in the ones place. If you still have questions about place value, review the section on Place Value in Module 30 - Adding Whole Numbers.

Whole Numbers:

When we count we use numbers. These numbers are called **whole numbers**.

0 1 2 3 4 5 6 7 8 9 are whole numbers. A person has two eyes. The number two is written as: 2. 2 is a whole number.

Whole numbers can be combined to make larger whole numbers. For example, 23 is a whole number. The 3 is in the one's place. It has the value of 3 ones. The 2 is in the ten's place. It has the value of 2 tens, or, 20.

<u>7</u> millions

<u>4</u> hundred thousands

<u>2</u> tens of thousands

<u>5</u> thousands

<u>6</u> hundreds

<u>3</u> tens

<u>0</u> ones

EXAMPLE: 7,425,630

Can you go higher? Of course!

SK 31 Subtracting Whole Numbers

The place of each number shows what the <u>value</u> of the number is. This continues on up as you add places.

Example: 1,350,987

How many hundred thousands are there in the number listed above?	
How many hundreds?	
If you were to put a 5 in front of the 1, what value would be assigned to the 5 placed there?	

Subtracting

Subtracting is just the opposite of adding.

Notice that these two questions really mean the same thing.

What is 5 minus 3?	
What number added to 3 equals 5?	

When you take things away from a set you are subtracting. Take 4 away from 5 and what do you get?

$$5 - 4 = 1$$

Working Basics

When you take 4 things from 5, you find 1 left. Take 6 away from 9 and what do you get?

$$9 - 6 = 3$$

Subtracting larger whole numbers follows the same principle. Remember to use place values. If there are not enough in the ones column to do the subtraction of ones, then you must borrow 10 from the tens place.

For example, take 3 away from 12 and what do you get?

$$12 - 3 = 9$$

Three (3) is larger than 2, so you borrowed one ten from the tens place and **added** it to the two. 1 **ten** + 2 **ones** equals 12. 12 minus 3 equals 9.

As the numbers get larger, you may have to borrow several times.

> Any time you subtract a larger number from a smaller number you must borrow from the next place.

Look at these examples:

A) Subtract 29 from 41 and what do you get?

```
         Borrow one
      3    1
       4 ——→1                          41
                      So we write    - 29
    -   2    9                         12
        1    2
```

SK 31 Subtracting Whole Numbers

9 is greater than 1 so you must borrow **one ten** from the ten's place and **add** it to the ones.

B) Subtract 106 from 905 and what do you get?

```
   borrow 1  borrow 1
      8 9    
      9̶ 1̶0̶ 1 5                9 0 5
    - 1  0  6      So we write - 1 0 6
    ─────────                   ───────
      7  9  9                   7 9 9
```

Since 6 is larger than 5, borrow one ten from the tens place. However, the tens place only has zero, so the tens place must borrow one ten from the hundreds place. This will make the hundreds place 8 and the tens place 10. Then the ones place can borrow one ten from the 10 in the tens place, making the ones place 15 and the tens place 9. Six (6) from 15 is 9. For the tens place, 0 from 9 is 9. Then in the hundreds place 1 from 8 is 7.

PRACTICE EXERCISE:

Try these exercises:

1)
$$\begin{array}{r} 236 \\ -42 \\ \hline \end{array}$$

2)
$$\begin{array}{r} 672{,}401 \\ -500{,}225 \\ \hline \end{array}$$

© Copyright 1990-2003   The Paxen Group, Inc.

3)   7,168
     -    561

4)   16,365
       -4,156

5) During the week of July 4th, Walt Disney World reported that 756,421 people visited the resort. Of that number, 314,121 were there on Saturday and Sunday. How many people were in attendance from Monday through Friday?

SK 31 Subtracting Whole Numbers

Did you remember to "borrow" when subtracting a larger number from a smaller number? Very good!

Remember....

Always line up the digits so the "ones" column is even. Subtract the "ones" column, then the "tens" column, then the "hundreds" and so on.

Also, remember that a zero is a number like any other number. Many mistakes in subtraction come from the zero. Treat the zero as you would any other number.

Quiz: SK 31 - Subtracting Whole Numbers

Name _____ Instructor's Initials _____
Date _____ Score _____
Competency Attained?   Yes_____   No_____

Subtract the following whole numbers.

1)   328
   - 103

2)   197
   - 46

3)   385
   - 165

4)   962
   - 328

5)   437
   - 229

6)   4,336
   - 257

7)   8,042
   - 5,206

8)   7,820
   - 3,436

Continued next page

9) 5,030
  - 1,173

10) 8,000
   - 7,891

11) 9,091
   - 439

12) 3,491
   - 37

13) 3,333
   - 3,324

14) 2,100
   - 109

15) 1,111
   - 222

Working Basics

Multiplying Whole Numbers

Basic Skills
Module SK 32

If your boss received a phone call from a client requesting that you double the order s/he placed yesterday, how would you calculate the new order? Or, suppose you were a chef who had to make a cake for a banquet of 150 people when the recipe serves 10. What would you do?

These are just two examples of how important multiplication skills can be in the workplace. Multiplication is a short way to find the sum of an item or number you need to add up two or more times. For instance, doubling the client's order would be done by multiplying each number by two, or adding it twice. No big deal, right? Adding is easier! In this case, maybe. However in the second example, all of the ingredients must be multiplied by 15. If there are 9 ingredients, each ingredient would have to be added together 15 times, unless you use multiplication!

If you can add you can also multiply. It takes a lot of time to list and add numbers like 8 sixes (or eight times 6). Therefore, it is much better to learn the answers to certain multiplication problems- at least all the one digit problems.

Working Basics

Here is a table which shows the answers to all the one-digit multiplication problems.

0	1	2	3	4	5	6	7	8	9	10
1	1	2	3	4	5	6	7	8	9	10
2	2	4	6	8	10	12	14	16	18	20
3	3	6	9	12	15	18	21	24	27	30
4	4	8	12	16	20	24	28	32	36	40
5	5	10	15	20	25	30	35	40	45	50
6	6	12	18	24	30	36	42	48	54	60
7	7	14	21	28	35	42	49	56	63	70
8	8	16	24	32	40	48	56	64	72	80
9	9	18	27	36	45	54	63	72	81	90
10	10	20	30	40	50	60	70	80	90	100

To use the table for these exercises:

◆ Find the row of one of the numbers you are multiplying (the rows go across from left to right).

◆ Find the column of the other number (the columns go up and down).

◆ Find the answer where the row and the column meet.

For example — to find the answer to 4 x 5:

◆ First — find row 4
◆ Next — find column 5
◆ Then, find where they meet.

THE ANSWER IS 20.

SK 32 Multiplying Whole Numbers

PRACTICE EXERCISES:

Follow the same steps to answer these questions.

What is:

1)   3
     x 9

2)   6
     x 2

3)   7
     x 8

Sometimes multiplying different numbers can give the <u>same</u> answers.

4) Use the table to find the answer to 4 x 4.   4 x 4 = ____

5) Now, find the answer to 2 x 8.   2 x 8 = ____

Working Basics

Is the answer 16 for both problems? If not, look again.

Look at the table and see how many ways you can multiply to get 12.

6) How many did you find? _____

7) How many ways can you multiply to get 24? _____

- ♦ REMEMBER—ANY NUMBER MULTIPLIED BY ZERO IS 0.
- ♦ ANY NUMBER MULTIPLIED BY 1 IS THE SAME NUMBER.

Write the answers to the problems on the next page as fast as you can—without making a mistake. Try not to look at the table. Look at the table only if you must.

PRACTICE EXERCISE:

1) 6x9 =	8) 5x6 =	15) 6x6 =	22) 6x7 =
2) 4x4 =	9) 1x5 =	16) 3x5 =	23) 7x9 =
3) 3x3 =	10) 4x9 =	17) 5x7 =	24) 4x8 =
4) 4x6 =	11) 5x6 =	18) 7x8 =	25) 3x7 =
5) 9x9 =	12) 7x7 =	19) 4x7 =	26) 6x8 =
6) 5x5 =	13) 5x8 =	20) 3x6 =	27) 8x8 =
7) 3x7 =	14) 8x2 =	21) 8x9 =	28) 9x1 =

Working Basics

> **The only way to become better at single digit multiplication is to practice and memorize these math facts:**
>
> ◆ <u>To multiply larger whole numbers</u> (ones with more than one digit), use the same principle. Always start on the right side of the problem.
>
> ◆ Always multiply the ones digit, then the tens digit and so on.
>
> ◆ Also use the principle of CARRYING over to the next place value (digit) as in addition.

Look at this problem.

◆ Step 1:

$$\begin{array}{r} {}^{+1}32 \\ \times\ 5 \\ \hline 0 \end{array}$$

Carry the 1 to the next place.

To finish the problem, you must:

◆ Step 2: Multiply 5 times 3 and add 1.

$$5 \times 3 = 15 + 1 = 16$$

Step 2:

$$\begin{array}{r} {}^{+1}32 \\ \times\ 5 \\ \hline 60 \end{array}$$

SK 32 Multiplying Whole Numbers

♦ Step 3: Put the 16 next to the zero. The answer to this problem is 160.

Step 3:

$$\begin{array}{r} {}_{+1}32 \\ \times\ 5 \\ \hline 160 \end{array}$$

Here is another example:
What will 9 sets of 20 give you?

$$\begin{array}{r} {}_{+1}\ 2\ 0 \\ \times\ \ 9 \\ \hline 1\ 8\ 0 \end{array} \qquad \text{Answer:} \qquad \begin{array}{r} 2\ 0 \\ \times\ \ 9 \\ \hline 1\ 8\ 0 \end{array}$$

Carry the 1 to the next place.

9 times 0 = 0 and 9 times 2 = 18. Carry the 1 and add it to the next column of numbers.

Finish these problems. The first step has been done for you.

$$\begin{array}{r} {}_{+1}83 \\ \times\ 6 \\ \hline 8 \end{array} \qquad \begin{array}{r} 21 \\ \times\ 4 \\ \hline 4 \end{array} \qquad \begin{array}{r} {}_{+4}56 \\ \times\ 8 \\ \hline 8 \end{array}$$

PRACTICE EXERCISE

Solve these problems.

$$\begin{array}{r} 45 \\ \times 6 \end{array} \qquad \begin{array}{r} 78 \\ \times 3 \end{array} \qquad \begin{array}{r} 34 \\ \times 4 \end{array} \qquad \begin{array}{r} 22 \\ \times 9 \end{array} \qquad \begin{array}{r} 98 \\ \times 3 \end{array}$$

© Copyright 1990-2003 The Paxen Group, Inc.

Working Basics

If the problem looks like this:

8 x 67 =

you must arrange it so the right side of the problem is even as in addition and subtraction, like this:

   67
x 8

PRACTICE EXERCISE

Answer these problems.

56 x 5 = _____

67 x 3 = _____

61 x 9 = _____

38 x 5 = _____

To multiply any one digit number times any number—no matter how large—you simply do the same thing over and over until you reach the end.

Increase 188 by 5 times and what do you get?

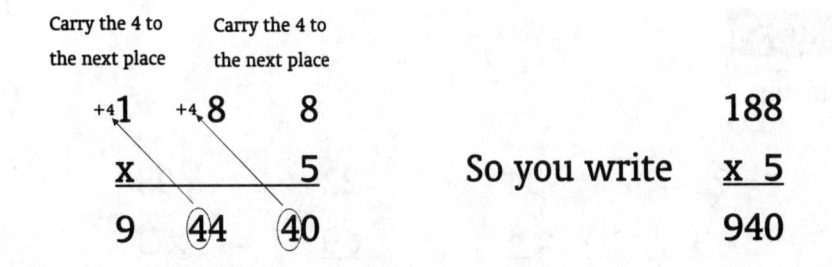

Carry the 4 to the next place	Carry the 4 to the next place			
+4 1	+4 8	8		188
x		5	So you write	x 5
9	44	40		940

SK 32 Multiplying Whole Numbers

Now, look at this problem.

```
  2964
X    8
23,712
```

- **First** — Multiply 8 x 4
- **Second** — Since the answer is 32, you place the 2 in the answer and carry 3 to the next place
- **Third** — Now, multiply 8 x 6. What is the answer? Add the 3 which was carried and you get 51. Put the 1 in the answer and carry the 5 to the next place.
- **Fourth** — Now multiply 8 x 9, add what was carried, place and carry.
- **Fifth** — Now, multiply 8 x 2, add what was carried and complete your answer.

Now, work this one.

```
56,890
   x 6
```

Practice these problems.

1. 8671 x 5 =

2. 5621 x 9 =

3. 4893 x 5 =

Working Basics

When multiplying multiple digits, multiply the farthest right number first, aligning it under that number. Then multiply the next digit to the left while aligning the factor directly under the number you are multiplying by, and so forth. Then add each set of multiplied numbers. For example:

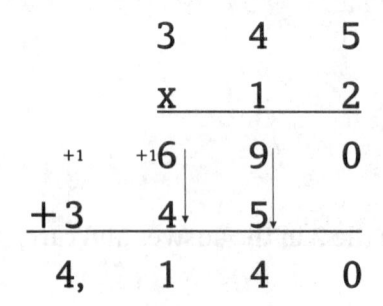

```
            3    4    5
       x    1    2
         +1  +16    9    0
       + 3    4    5
       4,    1    4    0
```

Notice how the problem is lined up. THIS IS IMPORTANT!

Always line up your answer below the digit by which you are multiplying. You complete the problem by adding. Begin on the right. Do not rearrange the problem. (Imagine there is a 0 below the 0.)

Here is a problem that has been partly worked, since the 76 has been multiplied by 4.

```
      76
    x 94
     304
```

- To finish the problem, you must multiply the 76 by the 9.
- Since 9 x 6 = 54, you place the 4 below 9 and CARRY the 5.

- 9 x 7 = 63, but you must first add the 5 which was carried.
- 63 + 5 = 68, so place the 68 next to the 4.

96

SK 32 Multiplying Whole Numbers

Here is the how the problem should look now.

```
    76
 x  94
   304
   684
```

Finish the problem. Remember to add without rearranging.

PRACTICE EXERCISE:

Okay, now try these exercises!

1.   86
     x   6

2.   24
     x 14

3.   387
     x   64

4.   3,697
     x 1,286

5. Mike Anderson drives a bakery truck from Orlando to Jacksonville every weekday. Each trip is 375 miles. Mike makes these deliveries 250 times a year. How many miles does Mike drive the truck each year?

Quiz: SK 32 - Multiplying Whole Numbers

Name _____ Instructor's Initials _____
Date _____ Score _____
Competency Attained?   Yes_____ No_____

Multiply the following whole numbers.

1.   24
   x   2

2.   32
   x   3

3.   304
   x   2

4.   837
   x   9

5.   7,010
   x   4

Working Basics

6.   3
  x   42

11.   28
   x   60

7.   8
  x   51

12.   30
   x   47

8.   76
  x   11

13.   364
   x   29

9.   85
  x   2

14.   830
   x   26

10.   64
   x   18

15. Jackie Jensen makes clay pottery. She completes 18 pieces per day and works 240 days per year. How many pieces of pottery can Jackie complete in one year?

Working Basics

Dividing Whole Numbers

Basic Skills
Module SK 33

Your supervisor is in a meeting and has left you in charge of completing an order that must go out today. There are 128 units that must be packed in eight crates for shipping. You must figure out how many units will be packed in each crate. To do this you must be able to divide. This is just one example of how division is used in daily life.

Division is a way to determine how many times one number is contained in another number. Using the example above, we need to know how many times 8 will go into 128 in order to put an equal number of units into the crates.

$$128 \div 8 = 16$$

ANSWER: 16 units will be packed in 8 crates.

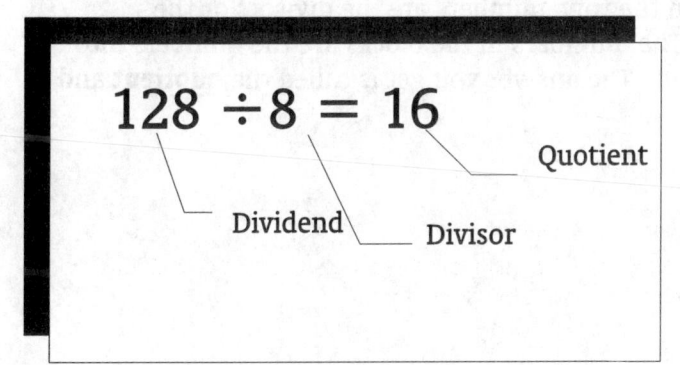

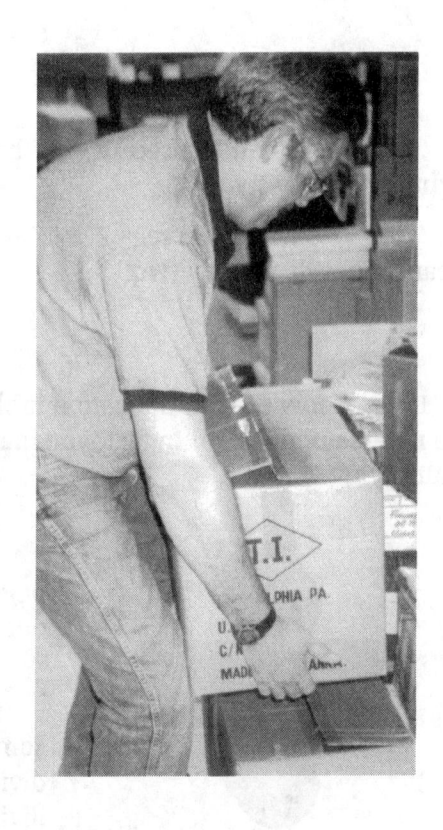

$$128 \div 8 = 16$$

Dividend — Divisor — Quotient

When you want to break up large groups of things into small groups you are dividing. Break up 8 into 2 groups of equal number and how many will be in each group?

8 divided by 2 = 4.

Working Basics

Break up 6 into 3 equal groups and how many will be in each group?

6 divided by 3 = 2. The answer is 2.

Division has 3 signs:

When you see: **8/2** this means eight divided by two.

When you see: **8 ÷ 2** this means eight divided by two.

When you see: 2)‾8‾ this means eight divided by two.

If you know the multiplication tables it will make division easier. Multiplication is the reverse of division! In fact, you may use the same table for dividing that you did in multiplying.

The multiplication table is shown on the next page. Look at it carefully and see if you can figure out how the table could be used for DIVIDING.

When you divide you are asking, how many complete sets of the **divisor** (the number you are dividing by) are in the **dividend** (the number you are dividing)?

When the table is used for division the row numbers are the divisors or the numbers by which you are dividing. The numbers in the blocks are the numbers into which you are dividing, or the dividend. The answer you get is called the **quotient** and is found across the top of the table.

SK 33 Dividing Whole Numbers

	0	1	2	3	4	5	6	7	8	9	10
1		1	2	3	4	5	6	7	8	9	10
2		2	4	6	8	10	12	14	16	18	20
3		3	6	9	12	15	18	21	24	27	30
4		4	8	12	16	20	24	28	32	36	40
5		5	10	15	20	25	30	35	40	45	50
6		6	12	18	24	30	36	42	48	54	60
7		7	14	21	28	35	42	49	56	63	70
8		8	16	24	32	40	48	56	64	72	80
9		9	18	27	36	45	54	63	72	81	90
10		10	20	30	40	50	60	70	80	90	100

Look at this problem.   56 ÷ 7

Find the ROW labeled "7".

Look across that row until you find 56.

Now, look up at the top of the column to find the quotient.

8 is the correct answer.

The table does not show all the DIVIDENDS you might want to use. Suppose you wanted to divide 7 into 59. Since 59 doesn't appear on the "7" row, you must use the next lowest number—which is 56. If you look up from the column with 56 you find that 7 goes into 56 "8" times with 3 left over. (59 minus 56 equals 3) This "left over" number is the remainder. When you write out the problem show your answer like this:

$$7 \overline{\smash{)}59} \text{8 remainder 3}$$
$$\underline{56}$$
$$3$$

Working Basics

> The remainder must always be less than the divisor.

Here are some practice problems. You can use the table to help you work them if you like—but try to think of the answers first. For example, with the problem 45 ÷ 5, ask yourself the question, "What times 5 equals 45?" Do this for each problem.

If there is a remainder, label it with a lower case r like this:

$$65 \div 8 = 8 \text{ r } 1$$

1)   54 ÷ 8 =

2)   50 ÷ 6 =

3)   49 ÷ 9 =

You can also do problems with larger numbers. Remember, no matter how long the problem, there are just THREE steps to follow. Follow these three steps over and over until the problem is finished.

The steps are:

         1. Divide

         2. Multiply

         3. Subtract

Continue until all the digits in the dividend have been used up. If there is a number left, it is the remainder. The remainder always has to be less than the divisor!

Here are the steps for this problem.

SK 33 Dividing Whole Numbers

$$932 \div 8 \quad \text{or} \quad 8\overline{)932}$$

1. DIVIDE

* Ask yourself, "Will 8 go in to 9?" Yes, 1 time. Put the 1 over the 9.

$$\begin{array}{r} 1 \\ 8\overline{)932} \end{array}$$

2. MULTIPLY

1 times 8 is 8. Put the 8 under the 9.

$$\begin{array}{r} 1 \\ 8\overline{)932} \\ \underline{8} \end{array}$$

3. SUBTRACT

8 from 9 equals 1. Put the 1 under the 8, and bring down the 3.

$$\begin{array}{r} 1 \\ 8\overline{)932} \\ \underline{8} \\ 13 \end{array}$$

Start again...

1. DIVIDE

Working Basics

Ask yourself, "Will 8 go into 13?" Yes, 1 time. Put the 1 over the 3.

```
    11
8 ) 932
    8
    13
```

2. MULTIPLY

1 times 8 is 8. Put the 8 under the 13.

```
    11
8 ) 932
    8
    13
    8
```

3. SUBTRACT

8 from 13 equals 5. Put the 5 under the 8 and bring down the 2.

```
    11
8 ) 932
    8
    13
    8
    52
```

Start again...

1. DIVIDE

Ask yourself, "Will 8 go into 52?" Yes, 6 times. Put the 6 over the 2.

```
     116
  8 ) 932
     8
     13
      8
```

2. MULTIPLY

6 times 8 equals 48. Put the 48 under the 52.

```
     116
  8 ) 932
     8
     13
      8
     52
     48
```

3. SUBTRACT

48 from 52 equals 4. Put the 4 under the 48. At this point there aren't any other numbers to bring down. Therefore, 4 is the remainder.

Working Basics

```
        116  r 4
    8 ) 932
        8
        13
         8
        52
        48
         4
```

Now go through the three steps for the following problem.

$$7\overline{)682}$$

1. DIVIDE

Ask yourself, "Will 7 go into 6?". The answer is no, so you must use the first two digits of the dividend (68). Next ask, "Will 7 go into 68?". Yes, 9 times. Put the 9 over the 8 in the quotient space.

$$\begin{array}{r} 9 \\ 7\overline{)682} \end{array}$$

2. MULTIPLY

Next, multiply 9 times 7. 9 times 7 is 63. Put the 63 under the 68.

$$\begin{array}{r} 9 \\ 7\overline{)682} \\ \underline{63} \end{array}$$

3. SUBTRACT

63 from 68 is 5. Put the five under the three and bring down the next number from the dividend, 2, to make 52.

$$\begin{array}{r} 9 \\ 7\overline{)682} \\ \underline{63} \\ 52 \end{array}$$

Start again...

1. DIVIDE

7 into 52. 7 can be divided into 52 seven times. Put the 7 over the 2 in the quotient.

```
      97
   7 )682
      63
      52
```

2. MULTIPLY

7 times 7 is 49. Put the 49 under the 52.

```
      97
   7 )682
      63
      52
      49
```

3. SUBTRACT

49 from 52 is 3. There is no other digit from the dividend to bring down. 3 is the remainder!

```
      97  r 3
   7 )682
      63
      52
      49
       3
```

SK 33 Dividing Whole Numbers

Work these next two problems by yourself.

$$5\overline{)9724} \qquad\qquad 2\overline{)345}$$

When the divisor has more than one digit, you use the same method you have already learned. Look at this problem.

$$155\overline{)364}$$

To begin, ask yourself, "How many digits in the dividend must be used?".

Say to yourself:

- ◆ "Will 155 divide into 3 one or more times?"
    - NO - 155 is larger than 3.
- ◆ "Will 155 divide into 36 one or more times?"
    - NO - 155 is larger than 36.
- ◆ "Will 155 divide into 364 one or more times?"
    - YES - 155 is less than 364 and can divide into 364 at least 2 times.

1. DIVIDE

Since 155 will go into 364 two times, place the 2 here.

$$155\overline{)364}^{\,2}$$

2. MULTIPLY

Multiply 2 times 155 and place the answer, (2 x155 = 310) under 364.

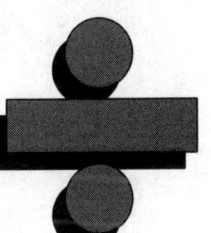

Working Basics

```
         2
155 ) 364
      310
```

3. SUBTRACT

Subtract 310 from 364. The answer is 54. At this point there is no other digit in the dividend to bring down. Therefore 54 becomes the remainder.

```
         2  r 54
155 ) 364
      310
       54
```

Finish these two problems:

```
      65                    8
6 ) 394                77 ) 668
    36                      616
```

SK 33 Dividing Whole Numbers

Remember! Multiplication is the reverse of division. Did you know that you can check your answer by multiplying it by the divisor to see if it is correct?

For example:

$$\begin{array}{r} 19 \\ 8\overline{)152} \\ \underline{8} \\ 72 \\ \underline{72} \\ 0 \end{array}$$

CHECK: 19 x 8 = 152

Don't forget to add the remainder when checking your answer.

PRACTICE EXERCISE

In the examples below, divide and check your answer:

1) 9)108   CHECK: 2) 7)536   CHECK:

3) 26)8681   CHECK: 4) 436)52,180 CHECK:

5. Mark and Joe are hiking the Appalachian Trail from Georgia to Massachusetts. They must travel 1,349 miles in 71 days. How many miles per day must they travel to accomplish this goal?

Quiz: SK 33 - Dividing Whole Numbers

Name _____ Instructor's Initials _____
Date _____ Score _____
Competency Attained?   Yes_____   No_____

Divide the following problems:

1) $804 \div 2 =$

2) $175 \div 5 =$

3) $792 \div 4 =$

4) $365 \div 6 =$

5) $7603 \div 8 =$

6) $364 \div 7 =$

7) $221 \div 4 =$

8) $603 \div 9 =$

9) $176 \div 20 =$

10) $53 \overline{)3922}$

11) $94 \overline{)38164}$

Working Basics

12) 38)$\overline{28100}$ 13) 81)$\overline{730}$ 14) 5)$\overline{167}$

15) Mary Anne has a collection of photographs. She has 2,961 photos she would like to place in an album. Each page of the album will hold 12 photographs. How many pages will Mary Anne need in her photo album?

Adding Decimals

**Basic Skills
Module SK 38**

Using decimals is essential if your job involves handling money, calculating percentages, or using the metric system. These are just a few examples that illustrate the importance of understanding decimals in the workforce.

Can you think of three specific jobs where using decimals is important? List them below:

Decimals, like fractions, are numbers that are broken into parts. A decimal point is used to separate a decimal (part or fraction of a number) from the whole number. Each place to the right of the decimal point has a value.

For example:

10.**1**   One place to the right of the decimal has a value of tenths. You read this as, **10 and 1 tenths.**

10.0**1** Two places to the right of the decimal has a value of hundreds. You read this as, **10 and 1 hundredths.**

10.00**1** Three places to the right of the decimal has a value of thousandths. You read this as, **10 and 1 thousandths** and it goes on and on.

Working Basics

Now practice reading decimals. Fill in the chart. Use decimals in your answer. The first one is done for you.

Thousands	Hundreds	Tens	Ones	Tenths	Hun-dredths	Answer
3	0	1	6	0	2	3,016.02
						5,991.3
0	5	8	0	8	0	
						9,013.89

Fill in the missing numerals in the sequence.

1. 4.5, 4.6, 4.7, _____, _____, 5.0, 5.1, 5.2

2. 100.01, 100.02, 100.03, _____, 100.05, _____

Adding Decimals

When adding decimals you use the same principles as adding whole numbers. Remember:

- ♦ Add numbers by adding the values in each place.
- ♦ When values exceed 9 you must carry over to the next place to the left.
- ♦ Keep decimals aligned to avoid errors.

SK 38 Adding Decimals

When adding decimals you use the same principles as adding whole numbers. Remember:

- Add numbers by adding the values in each place.
- When values exceed 9 you must carry over to the next place to the left.
- Keep decimals aligned to avoid errors.

Examples

$$\begin{array}{r}.2\\+.2\\\hline.4\end{array}$$

$$\begin{array}{r}.02\\+.02\\\hline.04\end{array}$$

$$\begin{array}{r}1.1\\+3.2\\\hline 4.3\end{array}$$

$$\begin{array}{r}2.5\\+.87\\\hline 3.37\end{array}$$

$$\begin{array}{r}.9\\+.2\\\hline 1.1\end{array}$$

Working Basics

PRACTICE EXERCISE:

1. John ran his leg of the relay race in 2.5 minutes. Mark finished his part in 3.1 minutes. Lewis completed the final lap in 2.1 minutes. What was their combined time for the race?

2.   13.86
  + 4.21

3.   6.46
  + 18.29

4.   847.010
  +118.911

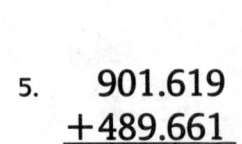

5.   901.619
  +489.661

Quiz: SK 38 - Adding Decimals

Name _____ Instructor's Initials _____
Date _____ Score _____
Competency Attained?   Yes_____   No_____

1.   37.66
    + 5.57

2.   12.95
       3.95
    + 3.25

3.   7.5
    + 6.1

4.   25.8
    +8.4

5.   109.3
    +1653.6

6.   374.6
    + .5

7.   21.71
    + 198.40

8.   1.295
    +.325

9.   1.234
    + 56.700

10)   17.99
      6.10
    +88.33

Working Basics

11)   1.95
   +66.31

12) 8,974.56
    675.22
    143.05
 + 510.18

13) 55.1350
    5.0826
  +1.4000

14) 39.600
    8.520
   20.747
 + 5.100

15)   6.67
  +14.06

16) 10.728
  +18.018

17) 11.70
   3.40
 + 3.25

18) 8.391
   3.999
 +2.417

19) 1.8018
 +2.8746

20) Josie Lincoln is a contender for the Olympics. She is competing in two timed events, the freestyle and the butterfly. Her latest timing in the freestyle is 3.45 minutes. She achieved 4.69 minutes in the butterfly. What is her combined timing for these two events?

Working Basics

Subtracting Decimals

Basic Skills
Module SK 39

Jack Schmidt is Production Coordinator for a company that manufactures printed circuit boards. Each board must be measured with a micrometer to determine width. The printed circuit board he just measured is 1.04 millimeters wide. It is supposed to measure .96 millimeters in width. How can he figure out the difference?

That's right! By subtracting .96 from 1.04.

Decimals, like fractions, are numbers that are broken into parts. A decimal point is used to separate a decimal (part of a number) from a whole number. Each place beside the decimal has a value.

10.<u>1</u>   One place to the right of the decimal has a value of tenths. You read this as, "10 and 1 tenths."

10.0<u>1</u>   Two places to the right of the decimal has a value of hundredths. You read this as, "10 and 1 hundredths."

10.00<u>1</u>   Three places to the right of the decimal has a value of thousandths. You read this as, "10 and 1 thousandths" and it goes on!

Now practice reading decimals.

Working Basics

Fill in the chart. Use decimals in your answer. The first one is done for you.

Thousands	Hundreds	Tens	Ones	Tenths	Hundredths	Answer
0	5	6	2	0	0	562
						1,347.89
1	4	6	5	1	2	
						991.9

Fill in the missing numerals in the sequence.

1) 25.6, 25.7, 25.8, _____, _____, 26.1

2) 989.97, _____, 989.99, 990, 990.1, 990.2, _____

Subtracting Decimals

When subtracting decimals you use the same principles as subtracting whole numbers. Remember:

- Subtract numbers by subtracting place values.
- When the values you are subtracting are greater than the amount you are subtracting, you must borrow from the next place value.

Examples:

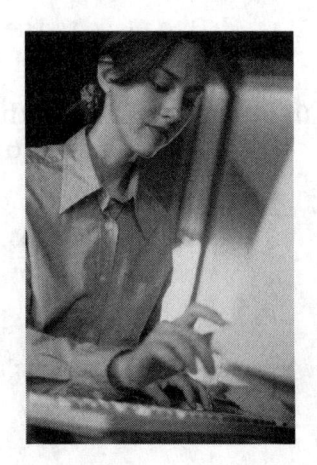

```
   .7
-  .2
   .5
```

```
   .15
-  .06
   .09
```

124

SK 39 Subtracting Decimals

```
   2.1
-  1.9
    .2
```

```
   6.85
-  1.9
   4.95
```

Figure out the answer for Jack Schmidt.

```
   1.04mm
-   .96mm
    .08mm
```

PRACTICE EXERCISE

Try some on your own.

1. Bobby is a member of the track team. His main event is the broad jump. During the track meet against Vanguard High School, his first jump measured 4.8 meters. His second attempt showed an improvement at 5.5 meters. What is the difference between these two jumps?

2.
```
    74.6
-   66.7
```

Working Basics

3.   801.46
     -   177.97

4.   491.606
     -    69.798

5.   811.010
     -   796.499

Quiz: SK 39 - Subtracting Decimals

Name _____ Instructor's Initials _____
Date _____ Score _____
Competency Attained? Yes ____ No ____

1. 1.00
   - .47

2. 124.00
   -   6.58

3. 675.22
   - 510.18

4. 1988.62
   -   99.87

5. 1649.9964
   - 1523.3600

6. 4.51
   - 1.79

7. 3435.613
   - 867.900

8. 153.81
   -   3.96

9. 21.7
   - 7.1

10. 4.900
    - 3.596

11. 33.64
    - 5.87

Working Basics

12.   1.242
    - .150

13. 199.78
    -   5.89

14. 116.40
    - 107.94

15. John is a truck driver in Munich, Germany. Every day he makes deliveries to either Stuttgart or Frankfurt. Stuttgart is 72.69 kilometers from Munich while Frankfurt is 131.89 kilometers from Munich. How much shorter is the trip to Stuttgart than the trip to Frankfurt?

Working Basics

Telling Time

Basic Skills
Module SK 82

You may think that telling time is a skill that everyone already has. Well, it may be, but because time is so important at work and in daily life, it's necessary to review.

A day is 24 hours long. There are 60 minutes in each hour and 60 seconds in each minute. The first 12 hours of the day start at one second after midnight and continue until 12 o'clock noon. These hours are called a.m. hours. The next 12 hours are those that start one second after 12 o'clock noon and continue to midnight. These are p.m. hours.

The position of the sun and the moon determine our time. Clocks were invented to make telling time more accurate and precise. Today clocks come in a variety of shapes and sizes. Most traditional clocks are round with the numbers 1 - 12 placed around the circle like this:

© Copyright 1990-2003   The Paxen Group, Inc.

Working Basics

Some clocks are square or rectangular, but the numbers are still placed in a circular pattern.

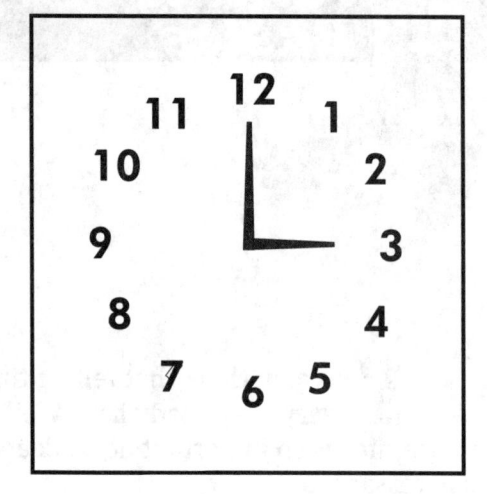

Both these clocks have "hands" or arrows that point to the time. The small hand or short hand points to the hour, which is one through twelve. These hours repeat twice a day. The big hand or long hand points to the minutes. The minutes are broken into 12 five-minute sections, or a total of 60 minutes. So if the big hand is pointing to the 3, then it is three five-minute blocks of time, or 15 minutes after the hour. If the big hand points to the 8, then it is eight five-minute blocks of time or 40 minutes after the hour. Often there is another hand that points to the seconds. It is usually long but thinner than the other hands.

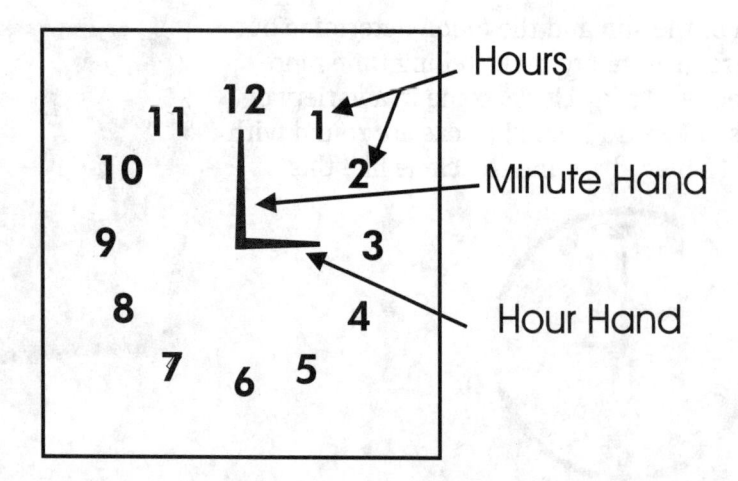

SK 82 Telling Time

Newer clocks give digital readouts. These make telling time very, very precise. If you have a clock radio, or a VCR, it may have a digital clock. The display window looks like this:

The display gives you the time. There is usually an indicator for a.m. or p.m.

Digital Clock

Some clocks use **Roman numerals** instead of Arabic numbers to represent the time. The numbers are still placed in a circular fashion around the face of the clock as in the example on the left.

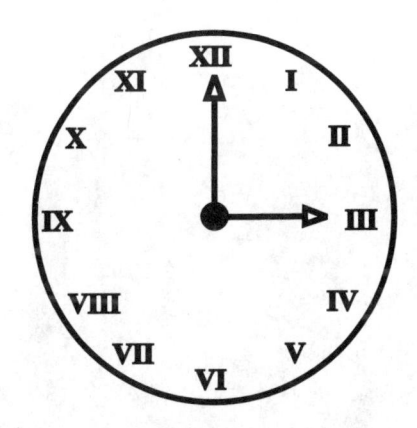

Clock Face With Roman Numerals

Other clocks use twelve marks instead of numbers 1-12 around the face of the clock. With these watches/clocks, one must be very careful not to confuse the markings. If necessary, starting with the first marking at the top of the face of the clock which represents the number 12, count clockwise by 1 to determine the number the mark represents.

© Copyright 1990-2003 The Paxen Group, Inc.

Working Basics

The clock on the left reads three o'clock. The long or big hand is pointing at the 12 and the short or small hand is pointing at the 3. There is no second hand on this clock. When the big hand moves past the 12, it indicates the number of minutes that have gone past the hour.

Look at the watch on the right. The big hand is pointing to 3 and the short hand is pointing to 2. Look closer. You will notice a thinner second hand on the third mark past the number 3. This indicates that 18 seconds have also past. Second hands are broken into 60 one-second blocks of time. Each thin line represents a second. In this picture the most precise time is 2:15:18.

So that is 15 minutes and 18 seconds after 2 o'clock.

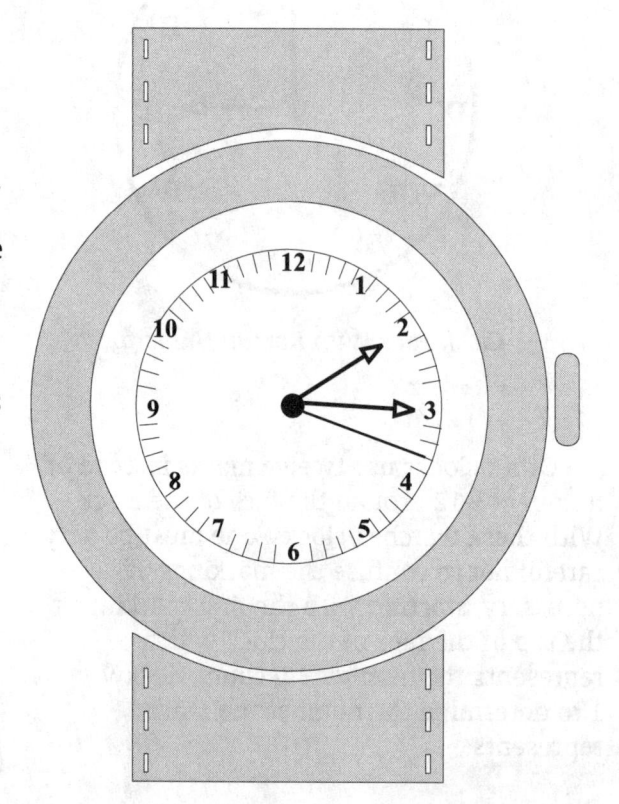

Try one more. The clock on the left says that the time is 4:45 or 15 minutes before five.

The little hand is between the 4 and 5 and the big hand is pointing to the 9 or the 45th minute mark. In 15 more minutes the big hand will be pointing at the 12 and the little hand will be directly on the 5. It will be 5:00.

Note that the small hand moves between the numbers as the big hand goes around the clock. The hour you read is always the last full number the big hand passed. For example, even though the small hand below is closer to the 5 than the 4, the big hand has not yet reached 5. So, the hour will be 4. The minutes are indicated by the long hand which is pointing to the 45 minute mark. The time is 4:45.

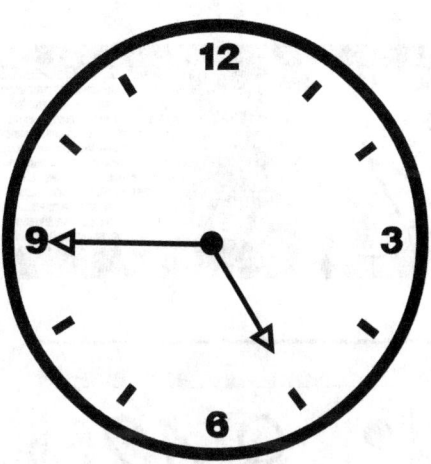

Working Basics

PRACTICE EXERCISE:

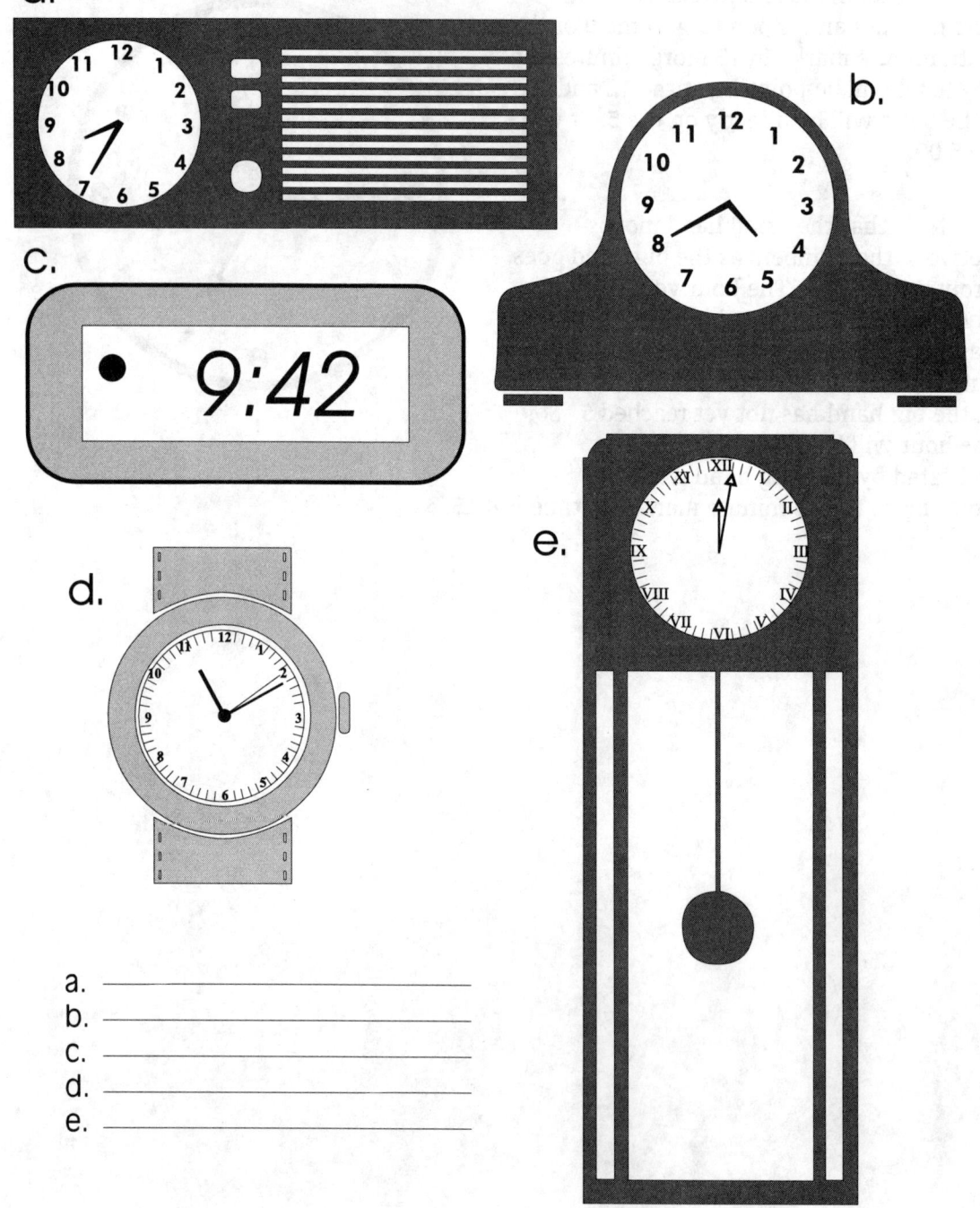

Practice telling time by reading these clocks:

a.

b.

c.

d.

e.

a. _____
b. _____
c. _____
d. _____
e. _____

Quiz: SK 82 - Telling Time

Name _____ Instructor's Initials _____
Date _____ Score _____
Competency Attained? Yes _____ No _____

Indicate the times shown below.

1.
2.
3.
4.
5.

1. __:_____
2. __:_____
3. __:_____
4. __:_____
5. __:_____

ANSWER THE FOLLOWING QUESTIONS. SPECIFY A.M. OR P.M.

6. If it is 7:30 a.m. and your boss asks you to meet him at the airport in 40 minutes, at what time should you pick him up?

   _____

7. If your customer joined the checkout line at 9:05 p.m. and has been waiting for 17 minutes, what time is it now?

   _____

8. You have a business appointment at 2:30 p.m. It will take you 1 hour and 10 minutes to get there. At what time should you leave so that you make it to the appointment on time?

   _____

9. If you can run a mile in 7 minutes and 35 seconds, how long will it take you to run 3 miles assuming you run at that same rate? (NOTE: Convert any seconds >60 to minutes).

   _____

10. If the movie starts at 3:10 p.m. and is 2 hours and 25 minutes long, at what time will the movie be over?

    _____

Working Basics

Allocating Time

Basic Skills
Module SK 85

Getting to work on time is one of the keys to job survival. Did you know that poor attendance and being late are two main reasons that employees get fired from their jobs? It is also the number one complaint employers have about the people who work for them.

Being on time shows the company that your work is important to you. It shows that you respect company policy and are committed. You've probably had to wait for someone before. Do you remember how you felt? Have you ever kept someone waiting? Have you ever had trouble keeping appointments or getting to places on time?

Once you know how to allocate your time, you won't have to worry about being late. It's really quite simple.

Allocating time means figuring out how long it will take you to do something or get somewhere, setting a schedule, and then following that schedule.

Next are some examples of how allocating time can be used.

To Determine Staffing

Managers of fast food restaurants use time allocation procedures to determine how many people are needed to work each shift. They estimate

Working Basics

the number of people who will be served and approximately how long it will take to serve each customer during that shift.

Example: *If you served 50 people during a 2 hour lunch shift and it takes 5 minutes to serve each, you will need 2 crew members.*

How do you figure this?

8:30 50 people x 5 minutes = 250 minutes = approximately 4 hours

4 hours of work ÷ 2 hour lunch shift = 2 crew members needed (each working 2 hours)

To Determine Departure Time

You may use the time allocation procedure to determine your departure or return time. For example, if it takes you 30 minutes to drive to work and you must be at work no later than 8:30 a.m., what time do you need to leave your house?

8:30 a.m. - 30 minutes - 8:00 a.m. depart time

You need to leave no later than 8:00 a.m. To be on the safe side, you really should leave at 7:50 a.m.

If your lunch break is at 11:30 a.m. and lasts one hour, what time do you need to be back at work?

11:30 a.m. + 1 hours = 12:30 p.m. return time.

As you determine when you need to leave for an appointment or meeting, don't forget to count the time that it will take you to get from one place to another. For instance, if you have a 2:00 p.m. appointment and it is a 10 minute bus ride plus a 5 minute walk to get there, what time should you leave?

First you add up the total travel time it will take you to get there:

10 minutes + 5 minutes = 15 minutes travel time
2:00 p.m. - 15 minutes = 1:45 p.m.

SK 85 Allocating Time

Correct answer: 1:45 p.m.

It is always good to allow yourself enough time for the travel there—otherwise you'll be late. It's always a good practice to allow 5-10 minutes extra time just in case you get lost or have a flat tire.

PRACTICE EXERCISES:

Answer the practice questions below.

1. Sandy is meeting her boyfriend Ricardo for lunch today at Maxine's Restaurant. Maxine's is a 5 minute walk from work. Sandy is allowed 45 minutes for lunch. She left her desk at 12:05. What time should Sandy leave the restaurant to get back to work on time?

2. Joe must be at work by 7:30 a.m. He gets the bus at Martin Road. From there it is a 20 minute bus ride to his stop at Bayshore Drive. Then he must walk 5 minutes to his office building. Using the bus schedule below, which bus should Joe take?

    a. Bus #6

    b. Bus #14

    c. Bus #10

    d. Bus #9

SCHEDULE - Transit Bus Lines
PICK-UP

Martin Rd.	Bus #
6:30 a.m.	6
6:45 a.m.	14
7:00 a.m.	10
7:20 a.m.	9

© Copyright 1990-2003   The Paxen Group, Inc.

Working Basics

3. Joey has a big presentation to make at work this morning at 7:30 a.m. He wants to get to work 35 minutes early. Which bus should he take? (NOTE: Use the schedule and times from problem 2.)

4. Mr. Joe of Wonderful Hamburger World expects to serve 100 for lunch. It takes an average of 5 minutes to receive an order, prepare and serve the food to the customer. Lunch lasts from 11:00 a.m.-1:00 p.m. (2 hours). How many employees does Mr. Joe need to work the lunch shift?

        a. 5

        b. 7

        c. 10

        d. 2

Quiz: SK 85 - Allocating Time

Name _____ Instructor's Initials _____
Date _____ Score _____
Competency Attained?   Yes_____   No_____

Answer questions 1-3 using the transportation schedule below:

SCHEDULE - Transit Bus Lines

PICK-UP

25th Avenue South	Bus #
6:10 a.m.	7
6:25 a.m	2
6:40 a.m.	4
6:55 a.m.	5

1. Terrance must be at work by 7:00 a.m. He catches the bus at 25th Avenue South. From there it is a 10 minute bus ride to his stop at Washington Circle. Every morning he buys a cup of coffee and a danish at a stand, which takes him 20 minutes. Then he walks 3 minutes to the hospital where he works. Which bus should Terrance take?

    a. Bus #7
    b. Bus #2
    c. Bus #4
    d. Bus #5

2. June also works at the hospital with Terrance and catches the bus at 25th Avenue South. She also must be at work by 7:00 a.m. It is a 10 minute ride to Washington Circle and it takes her 5 minutes to walk to the hospital. Which bus should June take?

    a. Bus #7   c. Bus #4
    b. Bus #2   d. Bus #5

© Copyright 1990-2003   The Paxen Group, Inc.

Working Basics

3. If June takes bus #5 and must be at work by 7:00 a.m., will she be on time?

    a. yes
    b. no

4. Your car pool ride picks up at 7:25 a.m. It takes you 45 minutes to get ready for work and eat breakfast. For what time should you set your alarm clock?

    a. 5:30 a.m.
    b. 6:00 a.m.
    c. 6:40 a.m.

5. Tom works as a newspaper writer. His story must be on his boss's desk by 2:00 p.m. for the next day's paper. If it will take 2 1/2 hours to write the story and he starts writing at 11:45 p.m., will he have the story in on time?

    a. yes
    b. no

6. Ms. Faye of Incredible Enchiladas is determining the work schedule for the lunch shift. She expects to serve 75 customers. Lunch lasts from 11:00 a.m.-1:00 p.m. It takes 8 minutes to serve each customer. How many crew members are needed to serve lunch?

    a. 2
    b. 3
    c. 5

7. It is a good idea to allow 5-10 minutes extra when allocating time just in case something causes a delay.

    a. True
    b. False

8. If Jordan's lunch break lasts 30 minutes, will he have time to walk 17 minutes to the newsstand to buy a paper and then make it back to work on time?

    a. yes
    b. no

9. You have an important meeting at 3:30 p.m. If it takes 12 minutes to drive there, 5 minutes to park your car and 7 minutes to get to the meeting place, what time should you leave?

    a. 3:05 p.m.
    b. 2:50 p.m.
    c. 3:15 p.m.

Working Basics

Identifying Work Related Problems

Basic Skills
Module SK 94

How many times have you heard someone complain about a problem on the job? Do you ever think, "Why don't they do something about it if the problem is so great?" Instead of complaining, energy and time could be spent on solving the problem.

There are many causes of conflicts at work. These are just a few:

- *Personality conflicts*
- *Inter-office politics*
- *Breaking the rules/violating company policies*
- *Misunderstandings*
- *Lack of communication*

An isolated incident in any of the above areas does not mean that there is a major problem. However, if conflict continues to occur, then you must admit that there is a problem that must be addressed.

Learning how to see and understand the causes of conflict will help you in your relations with people at home and at work. It will allow you to resolve conflicts before they get out of hand. Here are some examples:

❶ *Example:* Sheila and Jane have been friends ever since they began working at Sadies and Macs. Recently Sheila was promoted to supervisor in Jane's department. Since that time, Jane has remained distant from Sheila and avoids her if possible.

Working Basics

Jane (though she will not admit it) is jealous of Sheila's new position. She thought she should have been offered the promotion. On the other hand, she is sad because she feels she will lose Sheila's friendship now that she sees her hanging out with the other supervisors.

❷ *Example:* During staff meetings, John makes suggestions for almost every issue and comments on everything. He takes up time and bogs down meetings with his suggestions, many of which aren't even appropriate.

John's goal is attention. He wants others to notice him. The problem is his behavior annoys and irritates his co-workers and supervisor.

❸ *Example:* Susan, a co-worker who has been at the office for three months asks, "Where are the stamps kept?" Where does this file go?" "What should I do with this letter?" She doesn't seem to know where anything is or how to do anything on her own. She constantly asks others rather than finding out or doing something herself.

Susan is displaying inadequacy in her job as well as a bit of laziness. If you worked with her, you might feel frustrated.

The only way to remove a problem is to solve it. Think of a recent conflict you have had with a friend, relative, or teacher. What was the problem? How did you resolve it? Was it resolved appropriately?

_____

_____

144

When trying to solve problems on the job, consider these steps:

Steps for Solving Work Related Problems

STEP ONE:

Determine exactly what the problem is. Identify the problem from all sides by communicating with everyone involved.

STEP TWO:

Encourage all those involved to participate in finding solutions to the problem. Evaluate the different solutions. Comment on the positive and the negative sides to each solution.

STEP THREE:

Choose the best solution which is most acceptable to everyone. Some people may have to compromise.

STEP FOUR:

Put the solution into action. It takes active involvement and change in order to resolve a problem. How will the solution be carried out? When will it be done? Who will do what? These are the questions which must be answered in order to put the solution into action.

STEP FIVE:

Evaluate the solution after a period of time. Did it work? If not, find out what went wrong. Go back through steps 1-5 again until the problem has been resolved.

Working Basics

> **PRACTICE EXERCISE:**

Here are some examples of different work-related conflicts. Answer the questions using the steps to problem solving discussed above.

Situation: Jane shares an office with Richard. She is a very neat, organized person. Richard is just the opposite. He likes to spread out. His papers are always spilling over into Jane's work area. He leaves files lying around and can never find anything he needs. Jane is frustrated.

1. What is the conflict? _____

2. Who should be involved in finding a solution to this problem? _____

3. Which of the following would be the best solution to this problem?

   a. Jane quits her job.

   b. Jane offers Richard some assistance in getting organized.

   c. Jane files a formal complaint against Richard to her supervisor.

Situation: After reviewing the latest company telephone bill, the manager finds that Sam has been making long distance calls to his mother on the company line. This is strictly against company policy.

4. What is the conflict? _____

5. Who should be involved in solving the problem? _____

6. Which solution would be most appropriate?

   a. Sam agrees to write to his mother from now on instead of calling her.

   b. The manager fires Sam.

   c. Sam quits his job.

   d. Sam apologizes for violating the company policy, pays for the calls that he made, and agrees never to let it happen again.

Now check your answers:

1. Richard's work habits are bothering Jane and interfering with her work.

2. Richard and Jane.

3. b

4. Sam has violated a company policy - the manager must take action.

5. the manager and Sam

6. d

Quiz: SK 94 - Identifying Work Related Problems

Name _____ Instructor's Initials _____
Date _____ Score _____
Competency Attained?   Yes_____   No_____

Read the situations below and answer the questions.

> *Thomas was promoted to Supervisor. Since his promotion he has noticed a major behavior change in Tim and Alice, two employees who have worked for the company for a long time. They have been short with customers, late coming back from breaks and have missed several deadlines.*

1. What is the conflict?

   _____

2. Who should be involved in solving the problem?

   _____

3. Which solution would be most appropriate?

       a. yell at Tim and Alice in front of the other employees.
       b. ignore the problem, it will solve itself.
       c. meet with Tim and Alice to discuss the problem and try to find a solution.

4. If this solution does not work what should the Supervisor do?

   _____

> *Janet works for a magazine and is responsible for writing a regular column. She submits her article to the secretary each week to type for the editor. Lately, Janet has not been getting her typed work back from the secretary on time. The editor has been on her back for the material, which is late. Janet spoke with the secretary who said there was nothing she could do. Her attitude seemed stubborn and unpleasant, which is unusual for her. After talking with several other writers, Janet finds they are having trouble getting their typed articles returned on time too.*

5. What is the problem or conflict?

   _____
   _____

Working Basics

6. Who should be involved in resolving this problem?
    a. Janet
    b. the secretary and the editor
    c. The other writers
    d. All of the above

7. *After meeting to discuss the problem, the group finds that the secretary's work load has increased tremendously due to assignments she has been getting from another department.* What would be the best solution to the problem?
    a. issue the secretary a warning for not finishing her assigned work on time.
    b. hire a part-time assistant to reduce the work load.
    c. instruct the other department not to give assignments to the secretary when she is busy typing articles.

8. *You are a supervisor of All-You-Can-Eat Barbeque Grill. One of your oldest employees has been calling in sick quite a bit this month. You heard from one of the other employees that her mother is very ill and thus there is no one to keep the children.* What would you do?
    a. fire her when she comes in.
    b. talk to her to see if you can change her to the evening shift so she can retain her job.
    c. don't say anything. Let this behavior continue until one day she doesn't come back anymore.

9. *You and your boss misunderstand each other continually because she is a fast-moving person who never stops to listen for long. For example, she is so stressed out that she assumes she told you things she did not because she is muttering about them as she runs by you.* You should:

    a. speak to your boss about her behavior.

    b. ask her for a time to meet with her. Put this request and confirmation of the appointment in writing. At that time discuss the problem and propose solutions.

    c. go look for another job, quickly!

10. What is the final step in solving a problem?
    a. evaluate the results
    b. select the best solution
    c. identify the problem

Working Basics

Reporting Emergencies

Basic Skills
Module SK 95

An emergency is a sudden or unexpected happening or situation that calls for action without delay. Depending on the severity and nature of the emergency, action should be taken to prevent the situation from becoming worse.

If you are the first person on the accident scene:

- Do whatever is possible to get the accident victims with injuries out of any life threatening situations.

- Go for help or have someone standing call for help.

- Be prepared to tell emergency personnel the who, what, when, where and how of the accident (if possible).

- If there are medically qualified persons at the scene, allow them to take over medical treatment after giving them any information they may need.

- Try to secure the accident site as best you can so that more accidents do not occur.

- If vehicles are involved, check for gasoline or other fluid spills and don't let anyone smoke in the area.

- Update emergency personnel as soon as they arrive to assume responsibility at the accident site.

- **Remember:** Medical treatment should be provided to keep things from getting worse and **only** if you are qualified.

Working Basics

Should an emergency occur on the job, the steps are similar:

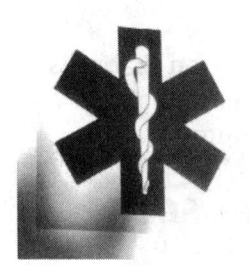

- Protect the individual from further injury (shut off machine, stop the bleeding).
- Go for help. Dial 911 (if available) or the operator for emergency assistance.
- Report the location, nature of the emergency and number of injured people involved. Request Police, Fire, or Medical Emergency Support.
- Keep the accident scene clear of bystanders, so that emergency personnel/vehicles have access and provide any information requested.
- Contact the Supervisor.
- Complete an incident report within 24 hours.

If you are involved in an accident that involves a fire, or a chemical spill, etc.:

- Move people away from accident site and do a head count.
- Report the nature of the incident. Also notify emergency staff of any missing persons.
- If a fire should occur and it does not look like it can be contained, get out immediately.
- Do not reenter the facility until emergency staff have given the all clear signal.

If you witness or are reporting an abduction, assault or theft:

- Be prepared to tell the emergency personnel the who, what, when, where and how.

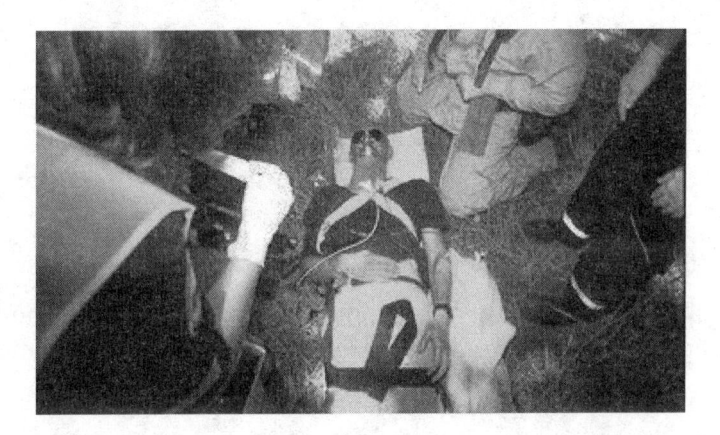

- Give the description of the victims and the persons committing the crime such as their height, weight (if possible), race, sex, clothing, etc. Make note of any special features which cannot be altered easily such as tatoos, scars, moles, etc.

- Give the make, model, year and tag number of the vehicle the individual(s) were driving.

- If a theft, give a description of the item(s) stolen.

- Give the direction in which the person or persons committing the crime were headed.

Working Basics

PRACTICE EXERCISE:

1. What is an emergency?

Answer:

2. In an emergency, what should you do if the area does not have 911 service?

Answer:

3. What should you do within 24 hours of an on-the-job accident?

Answer:

4. In the event of an abduction, theft, etc. what kind of information should you provide emergency personnel regarding the type of car used in the crime?

Answer:

Quiz: SK 95 - Reporting Emergencies

Name _____ Instructor's Initials _____
Date _____ Score _____
Competency Attained?   Yes_____   No_____

1. Should you follow basic medical procedures to ensure the safety of accident victims at an emergency scene to get them out of life-threatening situations?

   _____

2. If vehicles are involved in an accident, what should you check for? _____

   _____

3. What number should you dial to report an emergency? _____

   _____

4. If you witness an abduction, assault, or theft, what information will you need to give concerning the person(s) committing the crime?

   _____

5. What should you do if there is a chemical spill?_____

   _____

6. An on-the-job accident report must be completed within 48 hours of its occurence.

     a. true
     b. false

7. When reporting a theft, give a brief description of the items stolen.

     a. true
     b. false

8. If an employee has his/her hand caught in an operating machine, what should you do first?

   _____

9. If a building is evacuated during an emergency, what should you wait for before reentering the facility?

   _____

10. Under what condition should you attempt to contain a fire?_____

    _____

Working Basics

Reading Advertisements

Core Skills
Module SK 101

Every day we are bombarded with advertisements for products and services through the written media. The main purpose of advertising is to sell the product being advertised. For that reason, only the desirable aspects of a product are mentioned.

The motto, *"Caveat Emptor"*, or "Let the buyer beware" has applied ever since the beginning of trade between human beings. Buyers must make sure they are making a well-informed purchase. One part of being well-informed is reading advertisements carefully. That means read the fine print.

Try not to think of advertisements as "truth". Qualities may be exaggerated in order to get you to buy. Think of some of the big soft drink companies' TV commercials. They all say their products are the best. They are telling you what they want you to believe.

It is important that you read advertisements carefully. There may be a "hidden" message that is easy to overlook that could cause complications later. For example, a furniture company sale ad stated that you could buy now and not pay anything until January of 2001. However, in the last two lines of the ad, in fine print, was a clause stipulating that interest would accumulate at a 35% rate from the date of purchase. On a $1000.00 purchase, an interest payment of $350.00 would be attached! Not much of a sale, was it?

Comparison of written advertisements can help you find the best deal available. These two ads appeared in your local newspaper promoting the sale of compact discs.

Working Basics

1. Based on the wording of the advertisements below, which company appears to offer more CDs for the lowest total price?

Jams Music Services
Buy 4 CDs for
1 CENT!

plus shipping and handling ($5.98)
then buy 1 CD for $17.98 and

get another 3 CDs FREE!

RECORD HOUSE
Buy 8 CDs for
only 1 CENT!

plus shipping and handling ($1.85)
if you agree to buy 6 more CDs
at $14.98 each over
the next three years.

      a. Record House

      b. JAMS Music Services

2. What is the total price of the 14 CDs you'd receive from Record House if you choose to order the 6 CDs over the three years two at a time? (Remember to include the shipping and handling of $1.85 per purchase.)

      a. $23.00

      b. $24.95

      c. $91.74

3. What is the total price of the 8 CDs purchased from JAMS Music Services? (Remember to include shipping and handling of $5.98 per purchase.)

      a. $29.99

      b. $29.95

      c. $32.00

CSK 101 Reading Advertisements

Below are a few phrases and abbreviations with which you need to be familiar when reading advertisements.

ADVERTISING TERMS:

APR - Annual Percentage Rate
The yearly interest rate at which a borrower is charged for services rendered or products purchased on credit.

COD - Cash on Delivery
You must pay the delivery person for the product or service ordered before you can receive the product or service.

ALL LADIES, MENS & CHILDREN'S SHOES ON SALE

FOB - Free on Board
This is a term that identifies who is responsible for goods that are shipped and pays the shipping charges. Say goods are being shipped from Houston to New York. FOB Houston (Free On Board in Houston) means the buyer pays the shipping charges and is responsible for anything that happens to the goods on the way to New York. FOB New York means the seller pays the shipping charges and is responsible for the goods until they are delivered to the buyer.

Bait and Switch
This is an illegal method of advertising and selling in which the customer, initially interested in the product advertised, is persuaded to buy an alternative item. The salesperson usually begins to point out the disadvantages of the item on sale (the bait) and tries to switch the shopper to a higher priced item. *Caveat emptor!* (Buyer beware!)

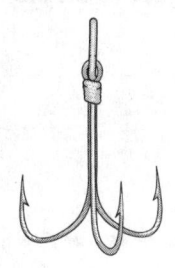

Two for One
This is a technique where businesses advertise products at low cost or even free. For example, "Buy a gallon of paint at regular price, and get the second gallon for one cent." The true cost of the second gallon of paint is not one cent. Chances are that the business is trying to

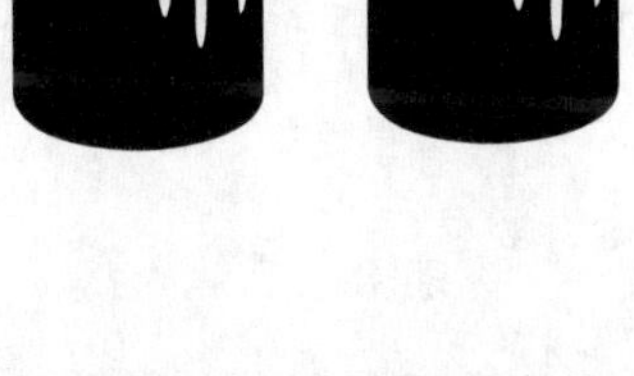

compete with some other company who is selling their paint at 50% off the regular price. Once again, *caveat emptor!* (Buyer beware!)

At Participating Stores

This means that not all of the company's stores may be having the sale.

Taxes Not Included

The price advertised does not have the state or local tax included, and the total amount you will pay will be more than the advertised price.

Limited Quantities

The store may allow you to purchase only a certain number of the sale items.

Some Restrictions May Apply

This means that there are specific instances in which the sale does not apply. You should ask ahead of time to find out what these are before you buy.

Subject to Credit Approval

This means that the store will not extend you credit until they have checked your credit rating and found it to be acceptable to them.

Other fine print to watch out for:

- Sales prices are available at participating stores.
- State and local taxes will be added where applicable.
- We reserve the right to limit quantites and to correct printing errors.
- Not all stores accept credit cards on advertised items.
- Bring this ad to receive sale price.
- Some restrictions may apply
- Offer subject to credit approval.

PRACTICE EXERCISE:

International Specials	
ROUND TRIP AIRFARES FROM ORLANDO	
LONDON	$549
FRANKFURT	$579
PARIS	$611
MILAN	$395
ROME	$426
Italian destinations require 2 people traveling together	
ORIENT/PACIFIC	
HONG KONG	$849
SEOUL	$899
TOKYO	$669
CONTINENTS TRAVEL INC. 869-0777	

GETAWAY TRAVEL (305) 445-9999	
EUROPE	
LONDON	$599
FRANKFURT	$649
MILAN	$769
PARIS	$659
ORIENT	
HONG KONG	$899
SEOUL	$979
TOKYO	$899
*HUGE SAVINGS ON BUSINESS AND FIRST CLASS * 7 YEARS RELIABILITY* *SERVICE IS OUR SPECIALTY*	

Compare prices. Which company would you use for a trip to:

London? _____

Paris? _____

Frankfurt? _____

Seoul? _____

Milan? _____

Did you notice there is a clause in the ad for Continents Travel regarding flights to Italy? Italian destinations require two people traveling together.

One Record Club advertises 8 CD's for one cent. Another will give you 6 CD's for one dollar. Both require that you purchase 6 more within a one year period. However, the second Record Club's prices are $1.00 - $2.00 lower than the first. To which Record Club would you subscribe?

Quiz: SK 101 - Reading Advertisements

Name _____ Instructor's Initials _____
Date _____ Score _____
Competency Attained? Yes_____ No_____

1. What is an advertisement? _____
   _____

2. Why do companies advertise their products or services? _____
   _____

3. What does the term, "caveat emptor" mean? _____

4. You went into a major department store to purchase an advertised 20" television for $199.00. The salesperson informs you that the television that is on sale is good, but not as good as the 20" television that sells for $250.00. What is this practice called?

   a. switch and bait

   b. bait and switch

   c. caveat emptor

5. Why is it important to read an advertisement thoroughly? _____
   _____

6. Aside from newspapers and magazines, where else can you find written advertisements? _____
   _____

7. What is comparison shopping? _____
   _____

8. What does "Offer subject to credit approval" mean? _____
   _____

9. What does it mean when an ad states, "We reserve the right to limit quantities."?
   _____

10. What does COD mean? _____
    _____